The Fly Fisherman's Streamside Handbook

The Fly Fisherman's Streamside Handbook

Revised Edition

by Craig Woods

Illustrated by
Robert Seaman

THE STEPHEN GREENE PRESS
Lexington, Massachusetts

First published in 1981 by Ziff-Davis Publishing Company
This revised and updated edition first published
in 1986 by The Stephen Greene Press, Inc.
Published simultaneously in Canada by
Penguin Books Canada Limited

Reprinted 1987, 1988

Distributed by Viking Penguin Inc.,
40 West 23rd Street, New York, NY 10010

LIBRARY OF CONGRESS CATALOGING IN PUBLICATION DATA
Woods, Craig.
The fly fisherman's streamside handbook.
Includes index.
1. Trout fishing.   2. Fly fishing.   I. Title.
SH687.W654 1986   799.1′755   85-27187
ISBN 0-8289-0576-2

Printed in the United States of America by
R. R. Donnelley & Sons, Harrisonburg, Virginia
Set in Times Roman

To my father

Preface

A YEAR AFTER THE FIRST EDITION OF THIS BOOK WAS published, I went fishing on Vermont's Mettawee River with my friends Sean Withrow and Pamela Tiernan. It was a gorgeous May afternoon, and we were hoping for a hatch of Hendricksons on the friendly little river.

As we were readying our gear, Pam, a novice angler, stuck a copy of *The Fly Fisherman's Streamside Handbook* into the inside front pocket of her waders.

"C'mon, Pam," I said, "just because you're fishing with me doesn't mean you have to carry that book along!"

"I use it a lot," she said. "I really do." I could see from the dog-eared cover and pages that it was true. That was a satisfying surprise.

Coincidentally, it was Sean and Pam, both of whom are in the publishing business, who took on the marketing of the first edition. Their efforts have met with such success that the ample first printing has been sold out. And so the pleasant task of preparing a second edition has fallen to me.

Any writer will probably tell you that a published work of his could be improved. It's that way with me. *The Fly Fisherman's Streamside Handbook* always satisfied me as an author and an angler, but after publication of the first edition I kept track of things I wanted to improve and add. There have not been a lot of changes, but those I've made for this edition have improved the book.

Primarily, I have updated the chapter on equipment to reflect innovations of the last five years; no major equipment changes have taken place, but new products reflect continuing refinement of our rods, reels, lines, and leaders. In the sections on fishing tactics and techniques I have

Preface

added bits and pieces here and there to improve the quality of the written instruction. New color photographs have been added, and I wrote a new chapter to fill in one gap in the original editorial offering: Nowhere in the first edition did we ever go fishing together! In the new chapter, "A Trip Astream," I try to show you how you can apply some of the techniques covered in the book to on-stream situations.

In the end, rereading and refining something that I wrote six years ago has been a pleasant experience. If I discovered that six years ago I split a few more infinitives than I do today, I've also discovered that the book achieved it's goal: to present the fundamentals of our sport clearly and accurately.

Acknowledgments

I WOULD LIKE TO THANK THE FOLLOWING INDIVIDUALS
for their help in this book: Pierre Affre, John Barstow,
Susan Dorgeloh, Dick Finlay, Jim Green, Gary Loomis,
Nick Lyons, John Merwin, Carl Navarre, Brenda Nellen-
back, John Randolph, Tom Rosenbauer, Jack Russell,
Paul Schullery, Ernest Schwiebert, Ed Van Put, Howard
West, Sean Withrow, and John Zahner.

I would like to thank the following tackle firms and
magazines for their help in assembling information for
this book: Fenwick/Woodstream, *Fly Fisherman* magazine, The Orvis Company, *Rod and Reel* magazine,
Rodon Manufacturing Company, Scientific Anglers/3M,
and UniRoyal.

Contents

Introduction   xiii

1. **Tackle**   1
   Rods, Lines, Reels, Leaders, Waders, Accessories

2. **Knots**   36

3. **Casting**   47
   Basic Cast, Roll Cast, Line-Mending

4. **Trout Streams**   60

5. **Trout**   65

6. **Trout Food**   67
   Aquatic Insects, Terrestrial Insects, Baitfish,
   Freshwater Crustaceans

7. **Trout Flies**   79

8. **Trout Stream Tactics**   85
   Fishing for Rising Trout, Fishing When No
   Trout Are Rising

9. **Playing and Releasing Trout**   92

10. **A Trip Astream**   95

11. **Trout Stream Etiquette**   99

    Index   101

Color Plate section appears after page 46.

Introduction

THIS IS A BOOK ABOUT FLY-FISHING FOR TROUT IN streams. It brings together basic information on fly tackle, trout streams, and trout. Its goal is twofold: first, to be a primer for the beginning fly fisherman; second, to be a reference for the more experienced angler. While this is a handbook that is designed to be carried in your fishing vest, it also provides armchair instruction.

If you're just getting started in this sport, I hope this book will help you develop basic fly-fishing skills and answer some of the many questions that will arise as you pursue the sport.

For the more experienced angler, I hope this handbook will be a source of useful information on topics ranging from tackle to stream entomology. The sport of fly-fishing, while intrinsically a simple endeavor, requires that you have a bundle of skills to call upon when the need arises. Once, for example, after traveling for most of a morning to an isolated slough in the Yellowstone Park area, one angler in our party admitted that he had to tie on a new leader but had forgotten how to tie a nail knot. I tied on his leader for him and we had an excellent day of trout fishing. If you're an experienced angler, I hope you'll keep this book in your vest as a source of information to answer such questions.

While most of the information contained in the following pages is directed toward fishing wadable trout streams, much of it is applicable to fishing for trout in lakes and ponds or while float-fishing the big rivers, and some of it is applicable to fishing for warm-water species, such as bass and panfish, and even to fishing for a few small salt-water gamefishes. This book, however, is not intended to

Introduction

be exhaustive in any of the areas it covers. It is basic in
scope, covering the skills and information you need to lay
a solid groundwork upon which to build further fly-fishing
skills.

The instruction and observations offered are the result
of my personal experience fly-fishing for trout in streams.
I have been at it most of my life, and I have had the great
benefit of knowing and fishing with some very good anglers. Rather than inundate you with exhaustive coverage
of each topic, I have chosen to present the basic information that I think will be most beneficial to you. For example, the tables that include information on tackle choices
are not steadfast rules of tackle selection; they are designed rather to give you a solid idea of the uses of different types and sizes of rods, lines, and so on.

A large portion of this book is devoted to tackle. It has
been my experience that many anglers, beginner and ad-
vanced angler alike, are sometimes confused by fly tackle.
In a book such as this I feel it important to explain carefully the nature and correct use of fly tackle so that the
beginner can start off on the right foot and the experienced
angler can clear up some misunderstandings.

Fly-fishing, to my mind, is one of the finest forms of
outdoor sport. And one of its greatest charms, I think, is
that to become proficient at it you have to become increas-
ingly conscious—and appreciative—of what's happening
in the world of your quarry. While in an immediate sense
the purpose of this book is to help anglers catch trout,
there is also a larger purpose to it: to help people appreci-
ate the natural world around them, a world from which
there is much to learn.

The Fly Fisherman's Streamside Handbook

1 Tackle

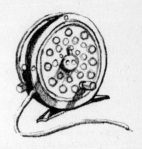

THE FIRST TIME I FISHED THE DELAWARE RIVER, which is an excellent trout stream in its upper reaches, I went with two companions. One of them is an angler who is about as expert at catching trout as you can get; the second is an angler who is, like myself, an experienced and knowledgeable fly fisherman. The expert was using a fiberglass rod that costs about twenty dollars, the second angler was using a bamboo rod that costs about eight hundred dollars, and I was using a bamboo rod that costs around one hundred dollars.

Our outing was cut short by a sudden downpour, but before we left the expert had taken two nice trout. The second angler and I had caught none. Part of the lesson here is that trout don't care about the brand name or cost of your tackle; the other part is that you needn't spend a lot of money to obtain effective tackle.

At its minimum, your fly tackle may consist of a rod, reel, line, leader, and a handful of flies. That's all you need to be in business on the stream. But you could own a battery of rods, several types of lines and reels, hundreds of flies, dozens of fly boxes, line and fly floatants, scissors, pliers, and a host of other things—each one of which could be useful on the trout stream. Whether or not to own a great deal of tackle is to a large degree a matter of personal taste; some people take a lot of pleasure in owning a fine rod or reel though they may fish with it infrequently. One thing is certain, however, and that is today's fly-tackle industry boasts such a variety of offerings that some guidance is helpful in finding the tackle that best suits your angling needs.

1

Tackle

Rods

The vital statistics of a fly rod are the material it's made from, its length, the line weight it casts, and its action. If you familiarize yourself with these aspects of a fly rod, you should be able to choose a rod that suits the trout-stream fishing you do.

Nearly all of the fly rods available today are made from one of four materials or composites of materials: bamboo, fiberglass, graphite (also called carbon-graphite or carbon-fibre), and boron/graphite. Rods constructed from any of these materials are suitable for trout-stream fishing, although the characteristics of each material may recommend it for different stream situations.

Bamboo rods are traditional and beautiful. While they are heavier than the synthetic-material rods and usually do not respond as quickly to the application of power by the angler, there is a distinctive feel in the action of a bamboo rod. This feel is hard to describe, but I would call it a liquid smoothness. With a good bamboo rod you feel as though you have smooth control over the line you're casting. Many anglers fish with bamboo rods because they believe this smooth control is important or adds enjoyment to casting, line control, and playing fish.

Fiberglass rods are the least expensive rods, and they are therefore a good choice for a beginner who is not sure how much time and money he wants to spend on fly-fishing. While they are inexpensive, there are excellent fiberglass rods available today, and they are by no means simply beginner's rods. Standard fiberglass rods are made from what is called "E-glass." A relatively new type of fiberglass is called "S-glass." An S-glass rod has more refined characteristics than does the standard E-glass rod, which is to say it casts better and otherwise performs the line-control functions of a fly rod better. S-glass is also lighter, and it is sometimes called "Hi-Mod" or "High-Density" fiberglass. S-glass rods are normally more expensive than E-glass rods. However, it is hard to determine

2

a substantial difference between trout rods made of E-glass and those made of S-glass, for the great value of S-glass is strength in rods made for fighting large gamefishes, such as tarpon, or casting a long line with heavy flies, as in some bass-fishing situations.

Graphite rods are lighter than bamboo or fiberglass rods, and they are usually quite powerful. Because of their lightness, they are excellent choices in the longer models. As well as being powerful, they can also be accurate and delicate, and they have the quality of quick flexural response when power is applied by the angler in casting, line control on the water, striking fish, and playing fish. Many anglers believe that graphite fly rods are the most efficient fishing tools available.

Innovations in graphite technology have allowed production of a sophisticated material called IM6 (sometimes referred to as "Graphite II"). IM6 graphite rods retain all the characteristics of "regular" graphite at a savings of seventeen percent in weight. Priced competitively, IM6 graphite rods are very efficient fly rods.

Boron/graphite rods combine the power and lightness of graphite with the hard-to-describe feel of bamboo. While they don't respond with the same quickness as graphite, boron/graphite rods can be extremely accurate and delicate casting tools. Boron/graphite rods, while displaying the smooth control characteristic of bamboo rods, have in addition a great deal of reserve power.

While the material from which a particular rod is made may suggest that it is a better rod than one made from another material, this is not necessarily the case. For example, there are inexpensive fiberglass rods that are superior to other, more expensive graphite models. Design is critical in the making of a fly rod, regardless of the material from which it is made.

Whether you choose a bamboo, fiberglass, graphite, or boron/graphite rod, you will have to find the right combination of length, line weight, and action for use on the streams you plan to fish.

When fishing on medium to large rivers, the longer the

Tackle

rod the better. A fiberglass or bamboo rod may be eight or 8½ feet long. Longer rods of these materials may become too heavy for comfortable casting; shorter ones tend to lack the power needed for casting. A graphite or boron/graphite rod may be eight to 9½ feet long (or longer) since the lightness of these materials allows a long rod to be manageable without being tiring. Most of the casts you will be making on medium to large rivers will probably be thirty feet (nine meters) or farther, and a long rod makes casting and other line-control functions easier at these distances. A long rod also allows you to hook the trout more easily when it strikes your fly, and it gives you more control when playing a fish.

When fishing the small, brushy-banked streams, a rod of seven or 7½ feet is about right. It can be made from any of these rod materials, although fiberglass and bamboo are preferable in these lengths. The shortness is required here because there simply isn't enough room to cast a long rod. In most instances, a rod need not be under seven feet for a small stream. On these streams you should try to use the longest rod that allows you to fish comfortably and effectively.

The variety and sophistication of rod models available today make it possible to choose almost any length of rod for almost any fly-line weight. (Fly-line weights are explained in the following section on fly lines.) While the length of rod is determined largely by the type of stream being fished, the line weight is determined by the size and type of fly being fished. Tables One and Two show suggested rod lengths for stream types and line weights for fly sizes and types. You should bear in mind, however, that the rods designed for the middle range of line weights, the six- to eight-weight lines, are generally easier to cast, and that the rods for the heavier line weights are easier to cast when it's windy.

Some rods may be rated by the manufacturer to cast more than one weight of line, and some rods may even be improperly rated by the manufacturer. An improperly matched rod-and-line-weight combination will be difficult

TABLE ONE: **SUGGESTED ROD LENGTHS FOR TROUT STREAMS**

Stream Type	Rod Length (feet)
Medium to large rivers, fast flow	8–9½, graphite or boron/graphite 8–8½, bamboo or fiberglass
Medium to large rivers, slow to moderate flow	8–9½, graphite or boron/graphite 8–8½, bamboo or fiberglass
Small to medium rivers, fast flow	7½–9½, graphite or boron/graphite 7–8, bamboo or fiberglass
Small to medium rivers, slow to moderate flow	7½–9½, graphite or boron/graphite 7–8, bamboo or fiberglass
Very small streams	7–7½, bamboo or fiberglass

and perhaps almost impossible to cast, especially for a beginner. Thus, it is very important that you try out a rod whenever possible before you purchase it to make sure that it casts the line weight it is supposed to cast. This will also help you determine if the action of the rod—how the rod behaves when you apply power to it—suits you. Not all nine-foot graphite rods for six-weight lines cast the same, and, of course, some are better than others, which is frequently not reflected in the price. Some rods flex more in the butt than others, some have stiffer tips than others. Some rods bend more in casting and take longer

TABLE TWO: **SUGGESTED LINE WEIGHTS FOR FLY SIZE AND TYPE**

Fly Size and Type	Line Weights
#2–#8, bulky or weighted	7, 8
#8–#12, bulky or weighted	6, 7
#10–#14	5, 6
#14–#26	4–6

Tackle

to respond than others, and the relative speed with which a rod responds is sometimes described as fast, medium, or slow action. Determining which action suits you is largely a subjective matter.

An alternative to purchasing a finished rod is to make one yourself from a kit. This does not mean making a rod from scratch; it means putting together the finished parts, and it's not difficult. Many manufacturers that sell finished rods also sell the same rod models in a kit form that includes all the necessary materials and components. Once you have learned how to build a rod, you've acquired the skills to make minor repairs on rods, such as rewrapping a thread winding or replacing a broken guide or a damaged cork handle. Building your own rod and making minor repairs yourself can save you a considerable amount of money.

In-season maintenance of the synthetic-material rods is a matter of cleaning. After you've fished with a rod for a while, the guides and the rod blank pick up microscopic dirt, and line floatant that you've put on the fly line may build up on the guides. When a wet line comes in contact with this dirt and grease, a tension is formed that slows down the line, which affects your casting. A mild, non-abrasive soap, such as liquid dishwashing soap, is all that's needed to clean the rod and guides—just wash with a sponge, rinse, and dry off. You might want to do this two or three times a season, or whenever you suspect the rod needs it. If you'd like to clean the cork handle on your rod, use the same soap, scrub with a toothbrush, rinse, and let dry. Nail-polish remover is also excellent for cleaning cork handles.

Bamboo rods require more attention than the synthetic material rods. If your bamboo rod has two tips, try to give each tip equal use during the season. Check the rod periodically for nicks and scratches in the finish that could require professional attention. Also, check for sets (improper curvature) in the bamboo, which can result from use. When playing fish, rotate the rod so that stress is not applied in the same direction all the time. Moisture can damage a bamboo rod (except those models that have been impregnated against penetration by moisture), so be sure to dry the rod thoroughly before closing it up in a rod tube. You can clean the rod in the same manner recommended for synthetic rods.

While most synthetic-material rods have an internal ferrule (male and female parts made from the same material as the rod blank, or rod shaft), bamboo rods normally have an external ferrule, which is made from a different material from the rod blank (usually metal). Check the ferrule on your bamboo rod periodically to make sure it is properly connected to the rod blank. If the metal ferrule doesn't slide easily into place, rub the male part with a bar of dry soap. You can clean metal ferrules with mild soap and water, using a cotton swab to clean the female part.

When joining and unjoining a rod, be sure to push and pull the sections apart in a straight plane. Never twist the sections or flex the rod when taking apart a rod. When putting the rod together, line up the guides before pushing the ferrule together—don't twist the joined rod sections to line up the guides. The closer your hands are to the ferrule, the easier it is to avoid twisting or flexing. If you can't unjoin a ferrule, have a friend place one hand on either rod section while you do the same, then pull in a straight plane. If alone, hold the rod sections behind your knees and pull apart by forcing your legs apart, pushing against your hands.

When walking to and from the stream, whenever possible hold the rod so it is pointing behind you. If you walk with the rod pointing in front of you, it's very easy to catch the tip on the ground or a tree and break it. When crossing a fence, place the rod on the other side, well away from where you plan to cross, before climbing over.

Clean your rods before storing them in the off-season, and in doing so you can check them for any repairs they might need. Store your rods in cloth rod bags inside sturdy aluminum or plastic tubes. Bamboo rods should be stored in a cool, dry place, and the top should be left off the rod tube so air can circulate to insure that no moisture will be

Tackle

trapped inside. To prevent sets in bamboo rods that may result from storage, the rod tubes should be stored standing upright, or the cloth rod bags can be suspended.

Lines

Some anglers say that the fly line is the most important part of a fly fisherman's tackle. Modern fly lines, which are made of a braided nylon core with a special plastic coating, will do things that anglers fifty years ago would probably not have thought possible. There are fly lines that float, sink slowly, sink quickly, or sink only in the tip portion of the line. There are lines that can triple your casting distance with the same amount of effort you would use to cast other lines. There are lines that are pale gray and others that are bright orange or fluorescent green.

The important features of a fly line are weight, taper, density, and color. Familiarity with these features will help you choose and use lines properly.

Fly lines are built in various weights, and each weight is given a numerical designation. The system of numerical designation was established by the American Fishing Tackle Manufacturers Association (AFTMA). Because the first thirty feet (nine meters) of a fly line is the part that's most often cast, it is this section that is weighed. Table Three shows the different line weights and their corresponding numerical designations.

Fly lines are offered in different weights because different weights of lines are necessary for different types of fishing, and consequently rods are designed for specific line weights. The line weights most often used for trout-stream fishing are four through eight.

Most fly lines are about ninety feet (twenty-seven meters) long, and within the first thirty feet (nine meters) or more a taper is incorporated in the plastic coating during the line's manufacture. This coating is decreased in thickness toward the tip to produce the taper. Lines are tapered to aid in casting and to allow delicate presentation of the

TABLE THREE: **FLY LINE WEIGHTS**

AFTMA Number	Weight (approximate)	
1	60 grains	3.9 grams
2	80	5.2
3	100	6.5
4	120	7.8
5	140	9.1
6	160	10.4
7	185	12.0
8	210	13.6
9	240	15.6
10	280	18.1
11	330	21.4
12	380	24.6
13	440	28.5
14	500	32.4
15	550	35.6

leader and fly. The different tapers available are level, double-taper, and weight-forward. Their respective abbreviations are L, DT, and WF. (Variations of the weight-forward taper are produced by some manufacturers as saltwater and bass-bug tapers.) Illustration One shows the configuration of the different fly-line tapers, including the shooting-taper line, which is described below.

The best use for a level line is when fishing very small creeks and streams where you have only a short length of line beyond the rod tip and a short leader. Most anglers will agree that for casting beyond very short distances, the double-taper and weight-forward lines are superior.

Tackle

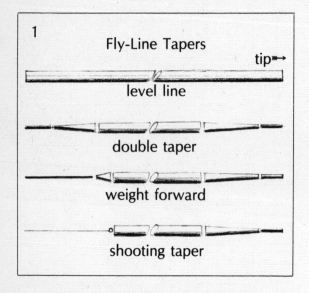

1

Fly-Line Tapers

tip→

level line

double taper

weight forward

shooting taper

The double-taper line has some advantages over a weight-forward line. It is easier to roll-cast and to control line on the water with one. It is also like owning two lines, because when one end of the line is worn out, the line can be reversed on the reel and the back end will be like new —seldom do you use more than half the length of the line when fishing trout streams. If you want, you can simply cut the line in half and attach the back end of one section directly to the backing line on your reel spool, storing the other section until you need it. (Backing line is small-diameter line that you put on your reel mainly to insure that if a fish runs farther than the length of the fly line you won't run out of line.)

While the double-taper has these advantages over a weight-forward line, many anglers prefer the weight-forward. The weight-forward design makes it easier to cast long distances. What you sacrifice to the double-taper line in line-control and roll-casting ability is not actually a great deal.

The different densities of lines are floating, intermediate, sinking-tip (the rest of the line floats), and sinking. Their respective abbreviations are F, I, F/S, and S. The different densities are designed to help you reach fish that are holding or feeding at certain depths. In most stream fishing, the lines you require are a floating line and a sinking-tip line with a ten-foot (three-meter) sinking portion in the tip. An intermediate line may also be of value. An intermediate line is designed to have a neutral buoyancy. If it is treated with line floatant it behaves like a floating line. Untreated, it sinks slowly. I often use an intermediate line interchangeably with a floating line because it is produced with a hard finish and in a narrower diameter, which allow it to land more delicately on the water's surface and cast easier. Table Four shows the depths at which these lines may be fished.

TABLE FOUR: **DEPTHS FOR FISHING DIFFERENT LINES**

(These are approximate depths in a stream of moderate flow. The depths will vary with current speed.)

Line Type	Depth
Floating	For fishing flies on the surface or within six to eight inches (fifteen to twenty centimeters) beneath the surface.
Intermediate	For fishing flies on the surface to two feet (sixty centimeters) beneath the surface.
Sinking-Tip (with ten-foot, or three-meter, sinking portion)	Two to six feet (sixty centimeters to two meters) beneath the surface.

Tackle

Color is the least important of the major features of a line, yet it shouldn't be neglected. There is some question whether a bright-colored line is visible to trout, and thus scares them, but most anglers agree that this is not so, or at least not to such a degree that it makes much difference. The best choice of color is light (such as white, cream, or peach) or bright (such as orange, yellow, or fluorescent green). You should choose a color that is most visible to you—which will help you control it better in or on the water and during casting because you can see how it's behaving.

The shooting-taper line (also called a shooting-head line) is a special line in which the first thirty feet (nine meters) of a weight-forward fly line are attached to monofilament or another small-diameter shooting-line, which is in turn attached to the backing. This line is designed to add distance to your cast, because the shooting-taper will pull the shooting-line quickly through the guides at the completion of a cast. It has limited application in trout-stream fishing, because casting long distances is rarely required. The abbreviation for the shooting-taper line is ST.

The most important features of a fly line—weight, taper, and density—are expressed in an abbreviated form. A WF5F line, for example, is a weight-forward, five-weight, floating line.

A fly line, like the rod blank and guides, picks up bits of microscopic dirt when it's used that cause it to slow down in casting by sticking to the guides and rod blank, and if it's a floating line the dirt will cause it to sink. Eventually, on any line, if this dirt is not cleaned off, it will shorten the life of the fly line.

In-season care of fly lines, as with rods, is thus a matter of cleaning. There are numerous fly-line cleaning products available today, many of which are silicone based and are applied to the line with a felt pad or a cloth, and, if you want, the line may then be wiped with another cloth or a paper towel. The cleaning preparations waterproof the line, leaving it a bit slick or greasy, which helps the line shoot through the rod guides and float. Additionally, a clean, high-floating line aids line mending and fish striking because there is less tension between the line and the water's surface. You can also clean your line with soap and water. You should clean your fly line whenever you feel it is not floating well or shooting through the guides well, which will usually happen after five to ten hours of fishing following cleaning.

Always be sure to keep the line free of any chemical that might be a solvent to the outer plastic coating. Most insect repellents, for example, will ruin a fly line if they come in contact with it. Another damaging solvent is gasoline. Avoid storage in the trunk of your car, because gas fumes will also harm the plastic coating.

If you own several lines and use them frequently throughout the season, you may keep them stored on the reels or spare spools you use them on, even during the off-season. If, however, you have a new line that you may not need for a year or two—until an old one wears out— keep it stored on the plastic spool on which it came from the manufacturer or coiled in about a three-inch (seventy-five-millimeter) diameter coil, keeping the coil intact with a couple of twist-on garbage-bag closures. Store it out of direct sunlight.

It's a good idea to mark each fly line according to weight, taper, and density. You can do this simply by marking the tip of the fly line with a waterproof marking pen. By devising a coding system of long and short marks, you can show these features of the line. You might, for example, use one long mark to mean weight-forward taper and two long marks to mean double-taper and a series of short marks for the weight (five for a five-weight line, six for a six-weight line, and so on). You can then use long marks again for density (one for floating, two for intermediate, and three for sinking-tip). Illustration Two shows how this system works. You can place the marks near the tip of the line so when the line is on a reel you can tell its weight, taper, and density at a glance. The long marks will be separated by short marks, so you need to remember

Tackle

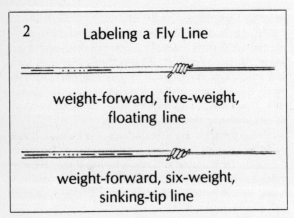

2   Labeling a Fly Line

weight-forward, five-weight,
floating line

weight-forward, six-weight,
sinking-tip line

whether the long marks closest to the tip of the line stand for taper or density.

This line-marking method is an alternative to using the press-on labels that come with fly lines and are designed to stick onto a reel or reel spool. These labels often come off. This line-marking method is also advantageous if you should take a line off a reel spool to store it for later use. Unmarked lines are hard to identify without being weighed and measured.

The proper reel-and-line combination should allow backing line to fit on the reel spool. Backing should be twelve- or twenty-pound (five- or nine-kilogram) test braided Dacron. Monofilament backing line is available, but unlike braided Dacron, it stretches when being wound on the reel under pressure and can later expand to ruin the reel spool.

Reels

While fly lines and fly rods have undergone extensive changes in recent years, the fly reel has stayed essentially the same for many years. It is possible to buy a fly reel that was manufactured before the turn of the century that will perform all the functions that modern reels perform.

It is sometimes said that the fly reel's primary function

14

is to store line. Unlike a bait-fishing or spin-fishing reel, the fly reel does not play an integral part in the basic fishing procedures of casting and retrieving. But a reel should do more than simply store line. It should have a drag (tension) system that allows you to strip line off the reel or play fish off the reel without overrunning the spool.

There are three basic types of fly reels available today: single-action, multiple-action, and automatic reels. In a single-action reel, one revolution of the handle results in one revolution of the spool. In a multiple-action reel, one revolution of the handle results in more than one revolution of the spool. In an automatic reel, a spring-loaded device retrieves line when you depress a lever, and you don't have to crank a handle to bring in your line. Both the multiple-action and the automatic fly reel have few advantages in trout streams. The appropriate fly reel for trout-stream fishing is the single-action reel because it adequately performs all of the necessary functions.

Single-action reels have very simple drag systems, and most of them have either a click-pawl or a brake-shoe system. Both are adjusted by means of a set screw, and generally the brake-shoe reels are adjustable over a wider range. However, the click-pawl drags are more than adequate for almost all trout-stream situations. Another kind of drag system is often available along with either the click-pawl or brake-shoe arrangements, and that is a palming drag. This means that the reel spool is exposed from the reel frame, and additional drag may be applied with your thumb or palm against the exposed spool. You apply this kind of drag when playing fish.

Either of these drag systems is adequate for trout-stream fishing, and the feature of greatest importance in a reel is workmanship—if a reel is not sturdily built you can easily ruin it by dropping it and possibly bending the frame to prohibit the spool from turning freely. A well-built reel will also have a smooth-working drag and winding systems.

A convenient feature of some fly reels is reversibility from right-hand to left-hand wind. The click-pawl reels

Tackle

are reversible quite simply, while the brake-shoe models require minor operations. But not all fly reels are reversible. Some anglers suggest that if you cast with your right hand, you should wind the reel with your left hand, and vice versa. If you hook a fish and must reel excess line in quickly—which is often the first thing to do after hooking a fish—you might have difficulty shifting the rod from one hand to the other and maintaining control of the fish. The first seconds after striking and hooking a fish are critical, and if you sacrifice rod control by shifting the rod from one hand to the other to reel in line, you're giving the trout an unnecessary edge. However, right-handed people may find that winding a reel with their left hand is awkward and therefore an inefficient way to retrieve line quickly. Use your own judgment when deciding whether to mount your reel for right-hand or left-hand winding.

Single-action reels are simple machines, and they require a minimum of maintenance. Largely, you must keep the reel clean to avoid corrosion, and you must lubricate the moving parts, which you should do according to the manufacturer's instructions. You should take care to keep the moving parts free from sand and grit that might enter, which dictate a thorough cleaning and relubricating if they do enter.

Spare spools are available for reels, and they are a good way to store a second line if you have one. You may, for example, have a rod that you use both a floating and sinking-tip line on, and when conditions dictate the use of one or the other, you simply can change spools. The spare spool can be kept in a fishing-vest pocket. Also, if you own one reel and have two rods that take different weights of line, with a spare spool you can use one reel for both rods. Put a wide rubber band around the line on the spare spool so the line doesn't begin to come off the spool in your tackle bag or fishing-vest pocket.

Most reels are rated by the manufacturer to hold a certain weight of line plus a certain amount of backing line. Fifty to seventy-five yards (forty-five to seventy meters) of backing is adequate for trout-stream fishing. However, the amount of backing should fill the reel so that, when the line is wound on top of it, there is only about a quarter-inch (six millimeters) of space not filled on the reel spool. This serves two purposes. First, with wide fly-line coils on the spool, more line is retrieved with each revolution of the spool than would be retrieved with narrow coils on the spool. Second, the line is better stored in wider coils on the spool, because if stored in narrow, tight coils it will have a greater tendency to retain those coils, thus tangling easily when in use as well as stressing the line's plastic coating.

If you're not sure how much backing you can fit on your reel, here's a method for putting on the right amount. You need two empty fly reels of the same size (you might borrow one). Attach the front end of the fly line to one of the empty reels and crank it onto the spool. Then attach the back end of the line to the backing, and wind the backing on until you've come within a quarter-inch (six millimeters) of filling the spool. Then cut the backing and attach it to the empty spool on the reel you want the line on, and crank the backing and line onto this reel.

When selecting a reel, check to make sure that the feet fit into the reel seat on your rod—most will do so comfortably, but there are some rod-and-reel combinations that don't fit.

Leaders

A leader is a tapered nylon line that you attach to the tip of the fly line. It is tapered to turn over from butt (heavy back end) to tippet (light front end) at the completion of a cast, landing on the water delicately to present the fly. The taper in a leader is imparted either during manufacture (which produces a knotless leader) or it is created by tying diminishing diameters of line together (which produces a knotted leader). Either type is fine for trout streams.

The proper length of leader and the proper tippet size are determined by current speed, water clarity, and, most

Tackle

importantly, size of the fly being used. Tables Five and Six show recommended leader lengths for different trout streams and recommended tippet sizes for different sizes of flies. Length and tippet size are the important dimensions of a leader, and they are normally expressed thus: a seven-foot, 4X leader (a two-meter, 4X leader).

You can buy finished leaders or you can tie your own. Leaders are usually inexpensive, and it may seem easiest to buy them already made up. However, since you have to know the knots for tying leaders in order to replace tippets and other sections of the leader, there is no special difficulty in tying up complete leaders.

In a later chapter on knots, three types of leader knots are shown: the blood knot, the double surgeon's loop, and interlocking loops. When you build a leader I recommend using blood knots or double surgeon's loops throughout until you reach the end of the section to which you'll attach the tippet. At the end of this section you can use a loop, and a loop in the back end of the tippet. When you want to replace the tippet all you do is cut the loop of the tippet and slip it out of the loop of the other section. The section behind the tippet stays intact; it is not shortened from tying knots. If you're on the stream and you want to replace sections behind the tippet, the double surgeon's loop is easier to tie and just as effective for trout fishing as a blood knot.

Illustrations Three, Four, and Five show three types of leaders—a leader on a sinking-tip line, standard leader tapers, and tapers developed by Pennsylvania angler George Harvey. Harvey's design is excellent for fishing dry flies and other patterns that must free-float on or near the surface. The Harvey leader lands on the water in a series of snaky curves that unfold during the downstream float to allow a free drift to the fly. The terms "hard nylon" and "soft nylon" in the Harvey leader illustration refer to the stiffness of leader material, which varies between manufacturers. The standard leader taper may be used effectively for dry flies as well as wet flies, nymphs, and streamers. Table Seven (p. 24) shows the metric equivalents of the measurements in the leader illustrations.

TABLE FIVE: **SUGGESTED LEADER LENGTHS FOR TROUT STREAMS**
(For Floating and Intermediate Lines)

Stream Type	Leader Length	
Medium to large rivers, fast flow	7½–9½ feet	2.3–2.9 meters
Medium to large rivers, slow to moderate flow	9½–10½	2.9–3.2
Small to medium rivers, fast flow	7½–9½	2.3–2.9
Small to medium rivers, slow to moderate flow	9½–10½	2.9–3.2
Very small streams	7½ or less	2.3 or less

TABLE SIX: **SUGGESTED TIPPET SIZES FOR FLY SIZES**

Tippet Size	Fly Size
0X	#2
1X	#4–6
2X	#6–10
3X	#10–14
4X	#12–16
5X	#14–18
6X	#16–22
7X	#18–26

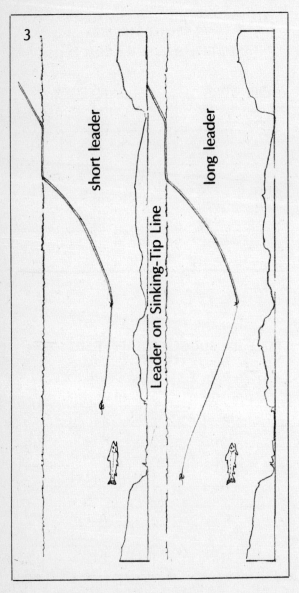

3 short leader long leader Leader on Sinking-Tip Line

4

Standard Leader Tapers

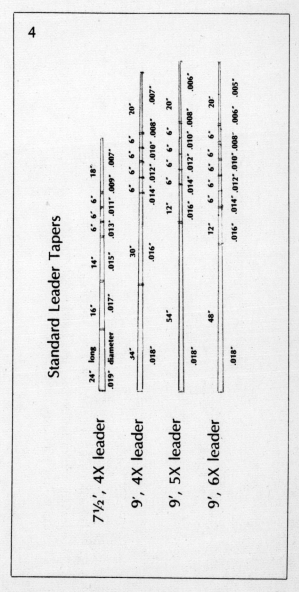

7½', 4X leader

24" long	16"	14"	6"	6"	6"	18"
.019" diameter	.017"	.015"	.013"	.011"	.009"	.007"

9', 4X leader

34"	30"	6"	6"	6"	6"	20"
.018"	.016"	.014"	.012"	.010"	.008"	.007"

9', 5X leader

54"	12"	6"	6"	6"	6"	20"
.018"	.016"	.014"	.012"	.010"	.008"	.006"

9', 6X leader

48"	12"	6"	6"	6"	6"	20"
.018"	.016"	.014"	.012"	.010"	.008"	.006"	.005"

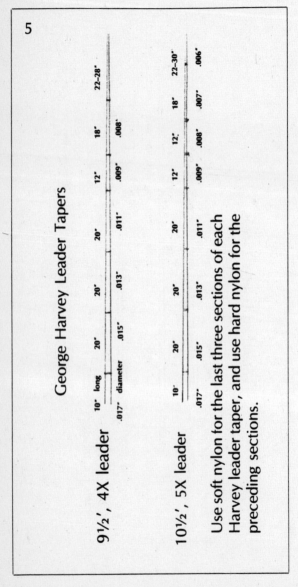

5

George Harvey Leader Tapers

9½', 4X leader

10" long	20"	20"	20"	20"	12"	18"	22-28"
.017" diameter	.015"	.013"	.011"	.009"	.008"		

10½', 5X leader

10"	20"	20"	20"	20"	12"	12"	18"	22-30"
.017"	.015"	.013"	.011"	.009"	.008"	.007"	.006"	

Use soft nylon for the last three sections of each Harvey leader taper, and use hard nylon for the preceding sections.

When using a sinking-tip line, you may use a very short leader. The sinking portion of the line will sink more quickly than the leader, and if the leader is too long, the sinking-tip section won't pull the fly down to the desired depth because monofilament tends to float. To make a leader for a sinking-tip line, no taper is necessary—a two- to three-foot (one-half to one-meter) length of heavy tippet material is sufficient (0X, 1X, 2X, or 3X material).

Leader material is marked in one or more of three ways to show size and strength: breaking strength (weight of pull at which it was tested for breaking), diameter, and X designation. Different brands of monofilament will have different relationships between breaking strength and diameter. The X designation is a measurement for diameter carried over from the days when natural gut was used for leader material, and it remains the term most often used by anglers to describe the diameter and strength of tippet material. The general relationship between these three measurements for tippet material is shown in Table Eight.

A recent innovation in leaders is the braided-butt leader from The Orvis Company, which has been available for just one season at this writing. The butt section of this leader is a multifilament nylon braid. There is no central core, making this an extremely supple-butted leader. The benefit is that power from your cast is efficiently transmitted from line to leader, which results in a leader that straightens easily and casts well in the wind. The supple braid allows a freer power flow than conventional, stiff, heavy monofilament nylon. Additionally, the braided-butt leader has little or no memory, which is a convenient feature. The tippet sections of the leader are standard light monofilament.

The braided-butt leaders are also available in sinking models from Orvis. The manufacturer offers leaders with three different sinking rates. The sinking capability comes from a narrow length of lead that is woven into the braid just ahead of the tippet. The sinking braided-butt leaders are really a refinement of the sinking-tip/short leader ar-

TABLE SEVEN: METRIC EQUIVALENTS FOR LEADER TAPER MEASUREMENTS

Standard Leader Tapers

2.3m, 4x (7½-ft., 4X) leader

61cm long	.48mm diameter
41cm	.43mm
31cm	.38mm
15cm	.33mm
15cm	.28mm
15cm	.23mm
46cm	.18mm

2.7m, 4X (9-ft., 4X) leader

86cm long	.45mm diameter
76cm	.41mm
15cm	.36mm
15cm	.31mm
15cm	.24mm
15cm	.20mm
51cm	.18mm

2.7m, 5X (9-ft., 5X) leader

137cm long	.45mm diameter
31cm	.41mm
15cm	.36mm
15cm	.31mm
15cm	.24mm
15cm	.20mm
51cm	.16mm

2.7m, 6X (9-ft., 6X) leader

122cm long	.45mm diameter
31cm	.41mm
15cm	.36mm
15cm	.31mm
15cm	.24mm
15cm	.20mm
15cm	.16mm
51cm	.13mm

George Harvey Leader Tapers

2.9m, 4X (9½-ft., 4X) leader		3.2m, 5X (10½-ft., 5X) leader	
25cm long	.43mm diameter	25cm long	.43mm diameter
51cm	.38mm	51cm	.38mm
51cm	.33mm	51cm	.33mm
51cm	.28mm	51cm	.28mm
31cm	.23mm	31cm	.23mm
46cm	.20mm	31cm	.20mm
56–71cm	.18mm	46cm	.18mm
		56–76cm	.16mm

Tackle

TABLE EIGHT: **TIPPET MATERIAL SIZES**

X Designation	Diameter		Breaking Strength	
0X	.011 in.	.28mm	6.5–10 lb.	3–4.5kg
1X	.010	.24	5.5–9	2.5–4.1
2X	.009	.23	4.5–8	2–3.6
3X	.008	.20	3.8–6	1.7–2.7
4X	.007	.18	3.1–5	1.4–2.3
5X	.006	.16	2.4–4	1.1–1.8
6X	.005	.13	1.4–2.4	.6–1.1
7X	.004	.10	1.1–2	.5–.9

Range indicated under breaking strength represents range of popular brands. Sizes above are generally consistent among brands.

rangement recommended earlier and shown in Illustration Three. But instead of having the heavy fly line within two or three feet of your fly, you have the less visible braided butt of the leader.

When used on a floating line, the sinking braided-butt leaders eliminate the need for split-shot or Twistons, and they cast better since the lead is distributed evenly over a twelve-inch section of the leader. You cannot, however, make subtle adjustments in weight as easily as you can with split-shot or Twistons, since you have to change leaders for a greater or lesser sink rate. In such a situation, experimentation with combining a braided-butt sinking leader with some split-shot or Twistons may prove effective.

On each outing to the trout stream, you should bring with you two or three spare leaders in the sizes that you expect to use. You should also bring along spare tippet material and material for the couple of sections behind the tippet in case you need to replace them on the stream. If you think your fly is not landing as it should or that it is not floating naturally on or in the water, the leader could be at fault. Don't hesitate to replace the leader or to re-place the end sections that may have grown short from tying knots.

Before beginning to fish you should remove the coils in the leader that result from storage on the reel or in a package. Some brands of monofilament have greater memory (tendency to retain a previous shape) than others. With some monofilaments it's enough to pull the leader through your hand. Lick or moisten the area of your hand that the leader is pulled through to avoid being burned or cut, and exert pressure as you pull it through. But be careful not to stretch the fine-diameter tippet, be-cause stretching it will cause it to kink and curl up. Other brands of monofilament will need to be pulled through a rubber pad, and inexpensive leader-straightening pads for fly fishermen are available from tackle manufacturers. However, a patch of rubber cut from a tire inner tube works well. Simply cut a piece large enough to double over the leader easily.

Most leaders are either clear or a light shade of blue or green. Heavily tinted leaders or leaders tinted various colors don't seem to camouflage the leader any better, or at least not enough to make a difference. However, lead-ers tinted for high visibility are sometimes advantageous because, as with a brightly colored fly line, they help you see the leader in or on the water.

Waders

There are three basic kinds of fishing boots for the fly fisherman to choose from: hip boots, chest-high stocking-foot waders, and chest-high bootfoot waders. If you won't be fishing in streams that are any deeper than midthigh depth, you might choose hip boots. But, it is unusual for most anglers not to wade in water deeper than midthigh depth, and if you are to own one pair of boots, chest-high waders are preferable to hip boots.

Bootfoot waders are normally made of fairly stiff mate-rial and the boots are built into the waders. They are eas-

Tackle

ier to get in and out of than the stockingfoot waders, and they are usually warmer. Stockingfoot waders are made of relatively light material and wading shoes must be worn over the feet of the waders. Compared to bootfoot waders, they are more comfortable to wear and to move around in, and they are easier to store or carry with you.

I feel that lightweight stockingfoot waders are superior to bootfoot waders. If they are light enough, you don't get hot and sweaty on the way to the stream, but most importantly your mobility in and out of the stream is increased. Ease of movement is an important safety consideration as well as an important comfort consideration. Lightweight stockingfoot waders provide less resistance to the stream's current when wading, and fatigue takes longer to set in. However, one important advantage of bootfoot waders is that they are usually made from tougher material than stockingfoot waders and they are more resistant to tears and punctures from sharp objects, such as barbed wire.

The proper fit in either kind of wader is important. With bootfoot waders a proper fit must be found in foot size and inseam. The foot size should accommodate at least one pair of heavy socks. If the fit is too small, wading and fishing can be uncomfortable. The inseam should be long enough to allow ease of movement, but not so long that it allows excessive bagging at the knees. If bootfoot waders bag at the knees, chafing will occur between your knees and the wader material will wear out prematurely in those spots. It's okay for stockingfoot waders to be baggy, even in the foot size, because the chafing incurred with these boots has minimal effect on the suppler wader material. Stockingfoot waders should, however, have a comfortable fit in the inseam to allow ease of movement.

When choosing a pair of waders, try them on and see how they feel walking up a flight of stairs, stepping over objects, sitting down, and during other movements that resemble those you will make on a trout stream.

The outer soles of bootfoot waders and wading shoes should have material on them to give you adequate traction while wading. Felt or polypropylene soles are normally a good choice, unless you're wading extremely fast streams or streams with very slippery rocks. For such wading situations you can obtain slip-on or lace-on traction devices that have metal studs or aluminum bars for traction. These super-traction devices usually are not very heavy, and once you get used to wearing them you may find you like to use them on all streams. Many manufacturers offer waders and wading shoes with felt soles already on them, and some offer metal-studded felt soles. When considering the extra expense of obtaining the right equipment for safe wading, the rule is better safe than sorry.

With stockingfoot waders you should wear one sock under the wader foot and another sock over the wader foot and under the wading shoe. This outer sock will prevent abrasion between the wading shoe and the wader material if sand or gravel should get into the shoe. If the outer sock is a calf- or knee-high tube sock (elasticized all the way up), after tying the shoelaces, fold the sock down over the tops of the shoes. This will prevent any sand or gravel from entering the shoe, and it will also help prevent the laces from coming untied while you're wading.

Basic wading technique involves positioning yourself sideways to the stream's current. You should use your upstream foot as the leading foot. With the leading foot, take a step, then bring the downstream, or following foot up to the upstream foot. When placing the upstream foot, be sure of your foothold before shifting your weight to it. When you are in the least unsure about your ability to cross a stream or wade through a stretch of stream, don't do it. Often, if you take the time to look around, you'll find that an alternative, safer route is available. Many wading mishaps are the result of carelessness or haste. It's a good idea to wear a belt around the tops of your waders, so if you take a spill water will be largely prevented from entering the waders. While a wading staff may seem an encumbrance at times, at other times it may be quite welcome.

When leaving the stream in wet waders or climbing

Tackle

over exposed rocks in the stream, you may find that some dry surfaces become instantly slippery when you place a wet boot on them. I have found, for example, that wet felt soles can be very slippery on ground covered with fallen leaves or dried grass.

When storing bootfoot waders in the off-season or between fishing trips, the best way is to hang them by the boots. Inexpensive boot hangers are available for this purpose. Don't store waders near electrical appliances or in a garage—ozone produced by electrical appliances and the elements in a car's exhaust will contribute to deterioration of the wader material. If you haven't got room to hang up bootfoot waders, fold them neatly with no unnecessary creases—the wader material will deteriorate quickly in spots where it is creased during storage. You should also avoid unnecessary creases with stockingfoot waders, either by hanging them up during storage or folding them neatly. Wading shoes should be allowed to dry before storing them.

If you take a spill in the stream or develop a serious leak in your bootfoot waders, there are several methods for drying them out. If you won't be using the boots for several days, it may suffice to hang them upside-down in such a way that air can circulate throughout the insides of the boots. If you want to dry them overnight, try stuffing them with crumpled up newspaper, removing the paper when it's wet. Repeat if necessary. Then hang the boots upside-down as described above. The quickest method, however, is to use a hand-held blow dryer. After removing as much excess moisture as you can, circulate hot air throughout the inside of the boots. You can also achieve this by attaching a vacuum-cleaner hose to the air exhaust of the vacuum cleaner, which will blow hot air.

The lightweight stockingfoot waders, because of the suppleness of the material from which most models are made, can be dried out simply by turning them inside-out. The lightweight vinyl stockingfoot waders now available will dry out in a matter of minutes if hung up so air can circulate around them.

Because waders are made from a variety of plastics and rubbers, manufacturers may have different recommendations for repairing leaks or tears in the waders. You should inquire when you purchase waders about the method for repairing leaks should they develop. The Orvis Company of Manchester, Vermont, sells a convenient emergency wader-repair kit. This kit consists of a stick of rubbery material that softens when heated over a match or cigarette lighter. It is then smeared over the hole. This provides excellent temporary repair for most waders.

An easy way to locate a hard-to-find hole in your waders is to take the boots into a dark room and shine a flashlight inside of them. Looking at the boots from the outside, you'll see light peeking through the hole. Don't, however, neglect to inspect the boots further after you've found one hole, because there may be more than one small leak.

Quite often, especially on warm days, condensation will form inside your waders while wading. The condensation will often be enough to dampen your pants, so if you suspect you have a minor leak in your boots but can't locate one, condensation may be the cause.

Accessories

The accessories you take with you on the trout stream are designed to make your fishing more efficient, easier, or more comfortable. In this category are fishing vests, fly boxes, clippers, sunglasses, hats, and so on. There is a plethora of different gadgets, even some gimmicks, that are designed for on-stream use by the fly fisherman. But you have limited space in your fishing vest, and the list below covers the essentials—and, actually, all you will probably need. If, however, you find an item that makes your fishing easier or more enjoyable, find a spot for it in your fishing vest.

Dry-fly box. This box should store flies in such a way

Tackle

that the dry-fly hackles are not squashed or otherwise damaged. Compartmentalized boxes are good, as are the boxes that have plastic ridges or slots into which you insert the hook of the fly, with the ridges or slots holding the fly securely in an upright position.

Wet-fly box. This box doesn't need to be compartmentalized, and it can be used for wet flies, nymphs, bucktails, and streamers. I have found that the boxes with metal clips or springs for holding the flies are unsatisfactory because you have to wrestle each fly in and out. Boxes with hard foam or plastic inserts for holding flies work well. Both the wet-fly and dry-fly boxes you choose should open easily and close securely.

Clippers. A pair of angler's clippers is used for trimming knots and sometimes flies. Most clippers come with a lever that works the clipper blades. Clippers can be suspended from a loop of fly line that is tied to a button-hole or ring on your vest. Small, pin-on, self-retracting reels are also available for this purpose. If you find that the clippers dangling from the vest get in the way, just put the clippers in a vest pocket when not in use (while still on the cord) or make a long cord and wear them around your neck, tucking the clippers inside the vest when not in use. If you don't suspend the clippers by a cord, you may drop them in the stream and lose them. Also, for convenience, the lever on most clippers can be removed and you can operate them simply by squeezing. A suitable pair of clippers is the kind sold for trimming fingernails, which can be purchased at a drugstore.

Forceps. Forceps (locking surgical pliers) can perform a variety of useful functions on the stream. However, the primary function is for removing a hook from the jaw of a fish you've caught. The forceps should be long enough to allow you to perform this function comfortably—if they're too short you can't see what you're doing because your hand is in the way, and it is also difficult to remove hooks that are deep in a trout's throat. Forceps may be suspended from the vest in the same manner as the clippers, and if convenient, on the same cord. The cord, how-

Accessories

ever, must be long enough to allow you to remove a hook from a fish comfortably.

Floatant. A small can of spray or paste fly floatant is handy to help float dry flies. I have found that the paste fly-line cleaner/floatants work well on flies, too. When applying this paste floatant to a fly, rub the paste first between thumb and forefinger to liquefy it so you don't make a sticky mess of the dry fly when you apply it. It is convenient to have the line floatant with you on the stream, because sometimes what you thought was a clean, high-floating line actually is dirty and needs dressing at streamside.

Split-shot or Twistons. These forms of lead weight are sometimes required to get your fly down deep, if that is where the fish are feeding. Split-shot are like BB's with slits in them so you can pinch them on the leader. Twistons are thin, lead strips that you wrap on and off the leader. When placed on the leader, either form of weight should be positioned about eight inches (twenty centimeters) above the fly.

Knife. A pocket knife with a short blade is needed primarily to clean fish that you have kept. The knife is a versatile tool, however, and you will find many uses for it. The Swiss Army style knives are popular among anglers. They may include, in addition to the knife blade, a corkscrew, scissors, screwdriver, and other useful features.

Leaders and leader material. Small spools of leader material in 0X through 6X should be carried with you. This size range includes monofilament for the sizes preceding the tippet in case you must rebuild a leader on the stream. Bring along two or three complete leaders in the lengths and tippet sizes you expect to use. The spools of leader material can be carried loose in a vest pocket or they can be put on a leader dispenser, which holds several sizes of monofilament in one container.

Leader straightener. The leader straightener can be suspended from the same cord as the clipper and forceps. Most straighteners available from tackle shops have a

Tackle

hole for this purpose. If you use a piece of inner tube for straightening leaders, simply make a hole in it to accommodate the cord.

Stream thermometer. A stream thermometer is used to check the water temperature of the stream. Such a check may reveal the water too warm or too cold, for example, for fish to actively feed on the surface. Knowing the water temperature can help you decide on stream tactics.

Hook sharpener. Many anglers don't realize how much more effective a fly hook is when it is sharpened periodically. The large, heavy-wire streamer and nymph hooks normally demand sharpening more often than the small hooks. Hook sharpeners are available at tackle shops.

Wading staff. This item may be termed "optional," and it is your own judgment that will determine whether you require one or not. Being realistic about the current speed and slipperiness of the stream bottom of the waters you fish as well as your own physical abilities will help you decide whether you should have a wading staff or not. It is a good idea to buy one, even if you may use it only occasionally on some streams you fish. Folding wading staffs are available that are lightweight, convenient, and safe.

Spare reel spool and fly line. If you're fishing with a floating or intermediate line, bring along a spare reel spool with a sinking-tip line on it. Then you can conveniently switch from one type of line to another should the need arise.

Net. While a net sometimes may seem to be an encumbrance, it's the best way to capture a fish. Make sure the net-frame opening is wide enough to easily accommodate a good-size trout, and that the net-bag mesh is knit closely enough so that a trout's head won't slip through and get caught at the gill covers. The net may be suspended by a clip from the ring attached to the back of the fishing vest. If a net you purchase doesn't have such a clip, a suitable clip can be obtained at a hardware store.

Hat. A hat protects your head from hooks if you make a bad cast, and it can also aid your eyesight. The brim should be wide enough to shade your eyes from the sun. A hat with a darkened underbrim helps to cut glare. Well-known angler Lefty Kreh says that if your fishing hat doesn't have a dark underbrim, you can blacken it with shoe polish. (Let the hat air out overnight after applying the polish, because otherwise the fumes from the polish will make your eyes water.)

Sunglasses. Polaroid glasses are an important aid to seeing fish and fish-holding spots, and they are also an aid to safe wading. They cut through glare to help you see the stream bottom. They also protect your eyes from errant hooks if you make a bad cast.

Flashlight. A small flashlight comes in handy for tying knots when the light is fading in the evening (which is often the best time to catch trout with flies) and for finding your way off the stream if you fish until dark. It should be small enough to fit in a vest pocket, and when you use it to provide light for tying knots, just turn it on and hold it in your mouth, which leaves both hands free.

The fishing vest in which you'll be carrying most of these items should have enough pocket space to do so. It should have a ring on the back for the net. The vest should allow easy access to pockets, and it should fit comfortably. A neutral shade—khaki or drab green—is desirable as it will be less visible to the fish that you're approaching than a brightly colored vest. The accessories that you should have in your vest are summarized in Table Nine.

TABLE NINE: **FLY VEST CHECKLIST**

Dry-fly box	Stream thermometer
Wet-fly box	Hook sharpener
Clippers	Spare reel spool and line
Forceps	Net
Floatant	Hat
Split-shot or Twistons	Sunglasses
Knife	Flashlight
Leaders and leader material	Leader straightener

2 Knots

USING THE CORRECT KNOT, PROPERLY TIED, FOR the right purpose is as important as any other aspect of fly-fishing. If a weak knot breaks while playing a fish, you've lost the fish, even though you may have cast like a champion to fool the trout.

The illustrations in this chapter show how to tie the eight knots that I have found necessary for trout-stream fishing. There are other knots that perform the same function as those that follow, but my criteria of ease of tying and suitable strength lead me to recommend these knots.

Whenever you tighten a monofilament-to-monofilament knot, be sure to moisten it before tightening it. You can do this simply by licking it. This way you avoid creating heat from friction when pulling it tight; the heat will substantially weaken the monofilament and the knot.

Stress from fish-playing and other fishing operations will fatigue a knot in the smaller sizes of monofilament. This applies especially to the knot you use to tie on the fly. This knot should be retied after three or four fish if you're using 5X or 6X monofilament for the leader tippet, and after every fish if you're catching large ones with tippet material smaller than 5X.

Backing to reel. This is a simple overhand slip knot. Place an initial overhand knot at the end of the backing to keep the end of the backing from slipping all the way through the knot when it is tightened.

Before you start this knot, remove the reel spool from the reel frame, run the backing through the appropriate spot in the frame or line guard, then tie the slip knot around the spool. Once the knot is pulled tight, the spool can be replaced on the reel frame and the backing cranked onto the reel. Remember that once the backing is tied onto

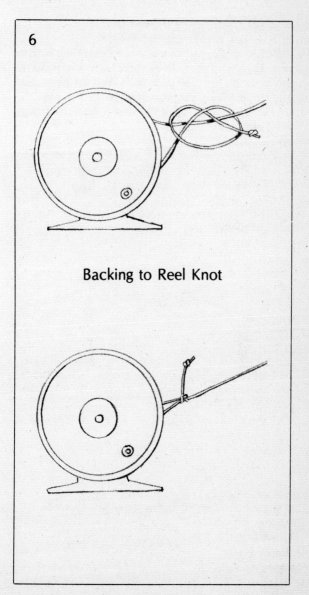

6

Backing to Reel Knot

Knots

the spool and the spool replaced on the reel frame, the backing must run through the frame.

Nail knot. The nail knot is used to attach the backing to the butt end of the fly line and the leader butt to the tip end of the fly line. The backing line and the leader butt may cut into the plastic coating of the fly line when the knot is pulled tight, but if the knot is neat and strong, that's okay.

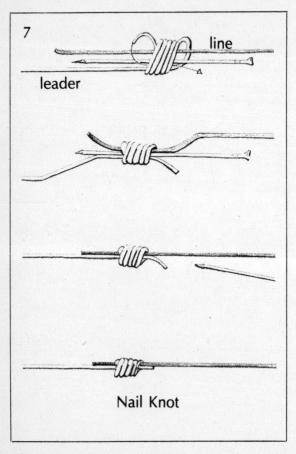

Nail Knot

Knots

The backing-to-line connection and the line-to-leader connection may be coated with a thin layer of pliable epoxy, such as the Wilhold glue previously marketed as Pliobond. This makes the connection smoother and somewhat stronger.

Some anglers prefer to use a splice knot for the functions for which I recommend the nail knot, but for trout-stream fishing I have found the nail knot adequate.

Blood knot. This knot is used to connect monofilament to monofilament, as when building a leader, and it makes a strong, small, neat connection. It also produces a straight-line knot (a knot in which the connected lines and the knot maintain a straight line instead of one line coming off the knot at a slight angle). I also use the blood knot to connect backing to backing when the need arises.

Double surgeon's loop. This knot performs the same monofilament-to-monofilament function that the blood knot performs. It is not quite as small and neat a knot as the blood knot, but it seems equally as strong. It is preferable for tying on tippets or rebuilding a leader on stream, because it is easier to tie than the blood knot. When you tie this knot, the lines that are pulled through the loop are the end of the standing line (line to which a new piece is being tied) and the entire new piece.

Making a loop and interlocking loops. Interlocking loops may be used to attach the butt end of the leader to a stationary leader butt of .017-inch (.43-millimeter) monofilament that is attached to the line tip with a nail knot. This stationary butt section may be five to ten inches (twelve to twenty-five centimeters) long, and by attaching the leader with interlocking loops, you don't have to tie a nail knot each time you replace a leader.

The interlocking loops may also be used to attach the leader tippet to the preceding leader section. A loop in the preceding section eliminates the need to periodically replace it as you make it shorter by tying knots to attach tippets. When you want to remove a looped-on tippet, cut the tippet loop and pull it through the stationary loop. The knots that result from the interlocking loops at the tippet

Knots

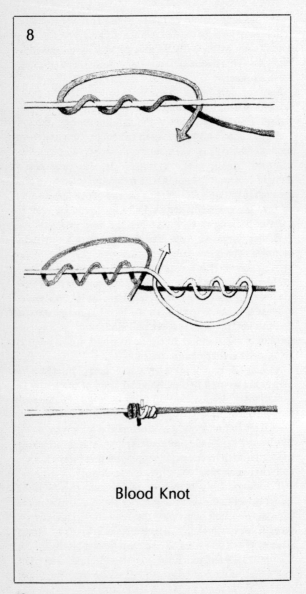

Blood Knot

9   tippet

end of preceding section

pull end of tippet and preceding section
all the way through

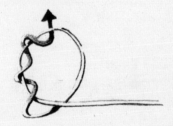

Double Surgeon's Loop

Knots

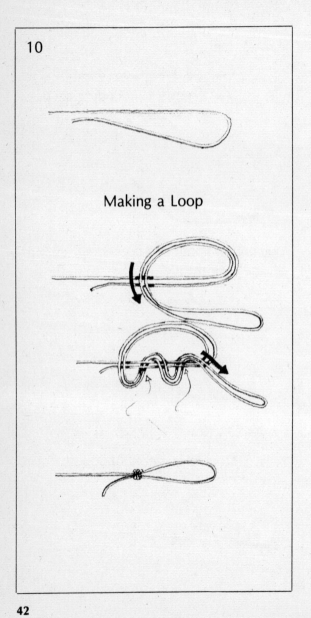

10

Making a Loop

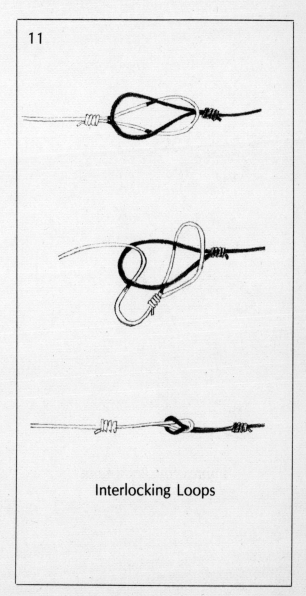

11

Interlocking Loops

12

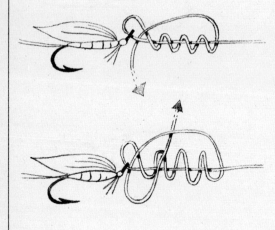

Improved Clinch Knot

13

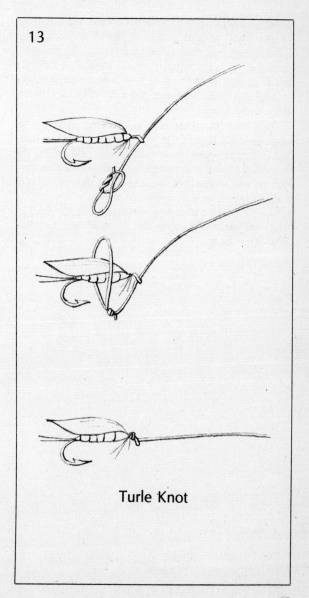

Turle Knot

Knots

are small and neat and do not affect the presentation of the fly and leader when they land on the water.

Improved clinch knot. This is a good knot for attaching large flies to large-diameter tippets because it makes a relatively neat connection. It is also easier to tie in the large-diameter monofilaments than in the smaller diameter monofilaments.

Turle knot. This knot is good for tying small flies to small-diameter tippets. The resulting knot is larger than that of the improved clinch knot, and it comes off the fly through the hook eye. Be careful when you tie the slip-knot portion of this knot, because if you tie it too tight it will damage the monofilament that is pulled through it. It will be pulled tight when you complete the knot. Also, the turle knot can more easily be tied by "feel" than the other fly-to-tippet knots.

3 Casting

FLY-CASTING IS MORE A MATTER OF TIMING THAN strength. It may help to keep in mind that most trout in streams are probably caught at a distance of less than thirty feet from the angler.

In the following instructions on casting, you should exercise your common sense in trying the casts. While the casts that follow are described as a series of individual moves, the end product of any cast should be the union of these moves into a smooth, easy stroke.

The hand with which you grip the rod is called your rod hand. The other hand controls the line and it's called your line hand. To grip the rod, place your hand around the grip, with the reel pointing toward the ground, as though you were shaking hands with the fly rod. This is the same grip that tennis players use for a standard forehand stroke. Your line hand will pull line from the reel when needed, and retrieve line after a cast. It should always be holding onto the line in a comfortable position in front of you.

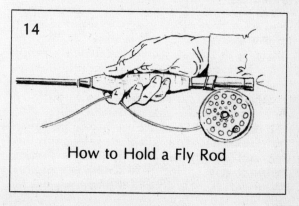

14

How to Hold a Fly Rod

Casting

Basic Cast

To make the basic cast, pull out about thirty feet (nine meters) of fly line and lay it in a straight line extending from the rod tip. (Practice this on your lawn or another such place.) Pick up the rod and hold it horizontal to the ground. Place the line under the forefinger of your rod hand, holding it firmly under your finger. Lift the rod slowly until all slack is out of the line, which should occur approximately at a forty-five-degree angle to the ground in front of you. In one smooth motion—fast and strong enough to pick up the weight of the line—bring the rod up and back until it is behind you at about a forty-five-degree angle to the ground. Keep your rod-hand wrist fairly stiff, and pivot at the elbow, with your line hand holding the line in front of you. Let the line land on the ground. Use only enough wrist motion to make the stroke smooth and comfortable. The fly line should now be laying out behind you. Bring the rod forward to its original position and let the line land again. Practice this until you feel comfortable and in control of the motion.

You are now ready to do the same thing but without letting the line land on the ground on the backcast. You still want to stop the rod at the forty-five degree angle behind you, but instead of letting the line fall to the ground, you bring the rod and line forward again. Don't bring the rod forward until the line has just about straightened out in the air behind you. You will have to hesitate to allow the line to straighten out behind you. Watch the line in the air and time your forward stroke accordingly. When you come forward again bring the rod to the horizontal position and let the line drop to the ground. Practice this until you can make the line lay out straight in front of you after the single backcast.

Now, instead of letting the line drop on the forward cast, you can try to do a series of false casts (forward and backward casts keeping the line in the air). In a smooth motion bring the rod back to the forty-five-degree angle, let the line almost straighten out behind you, bring it

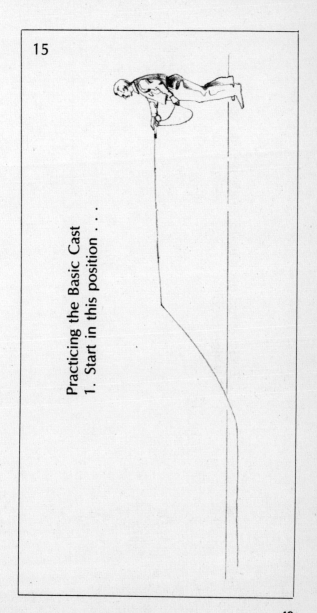

15

Practicing the Basic Cast
1. Start in this position . . .

Casting

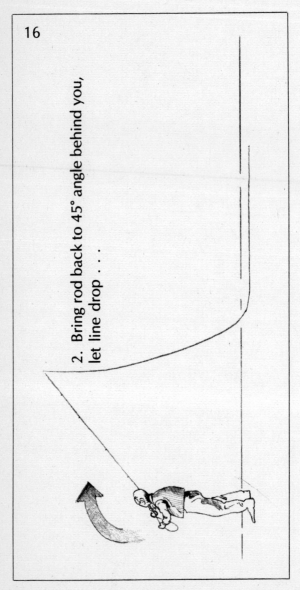

16

2. Bring rod back to 45° angle behind you, let line drop . . . .

17

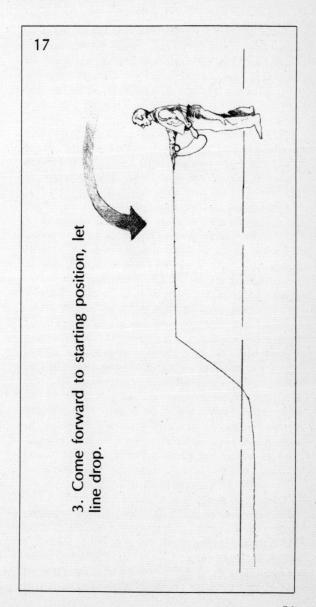

3. Come forward to starting position, let line drop.

Casting

smoothly forward again—but this time stop the rod in the forward position at forty-five degrees to the ground. Wait for the line almost to straighten in front of you—watch the line—then bring the rod behind you again. Practice this, making three or four false casts before letting the line drop in front of you. Keep practicing until you feel comfortable and in control of the rod and line.

Now try it with twenty feet (six meters) of line, and then forty feet (twelve meters). You will see that you have to make minor adjustments in the amount of power you apply and in your timing to handle different lengths of line.

False-casting is used between presentations of the fly to either dry off a dry fly, change the direction of the cast, or lengthen the cast by shooting line in the air. Remember, when you are in a fishing situation and find yourself false-casting for no reason (which is common among many anglers), you are affecting your efficiency as a fisherman. As the saying goes, it's easier to catch fish with your fly in the water than it is with your fly in the air.

Now you are ready to learn how to lengthen your cast by shooting line. Shooting line means that when you come forward with the rod, as the line straightens out in front of you, you let more line be pulled—or shot—through the rod guides. You may, for example, have thirty feet (nine meters) of line out in front of you and want to make a cast of forty feet (twelve meters). To do this, you would pick up the line, make a single backcast, and when the line came forward you would let the extra ten feet (three meters) go through the guides to land at forty feet (twelve meters). You must have the extra ten feet (three meters) of line pulled off the reel, ready to be shot out.

To practice shooting line, pull out about thirty feet (nine meters) of line in a straight line in front of you. Strip ten feet (three meters) of line from the reel, letting it lay on the ground in front of you. Bring the rod up until slack is out, backcast, stopping at the forty-five-degree angle, and come forward to a forty-five-degree angle in front of you. When the line has almost straightened out in front of

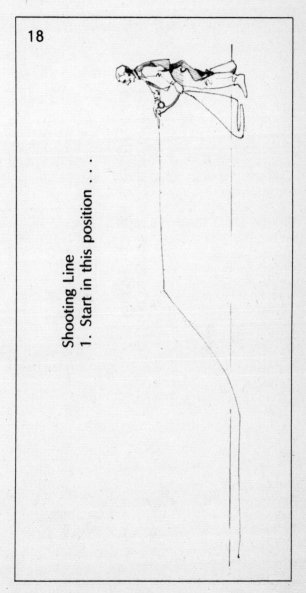

18

Shooting Line
1. Start in this position . . . .

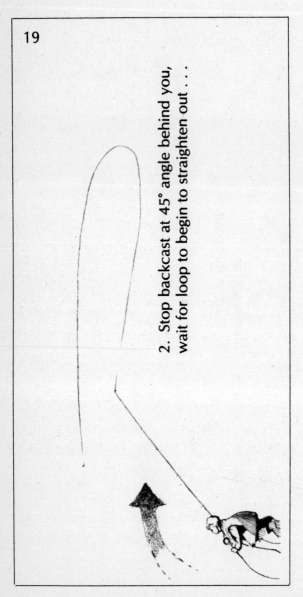

19

2. Stop backcast at 45° angle behind you,
wait for loop to begin to straighten out . . .

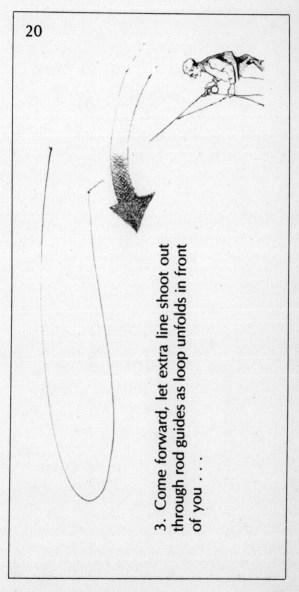

20

3. Come forward, let extra line shoot out through rod guides as loop unfolds in front of you . . . .

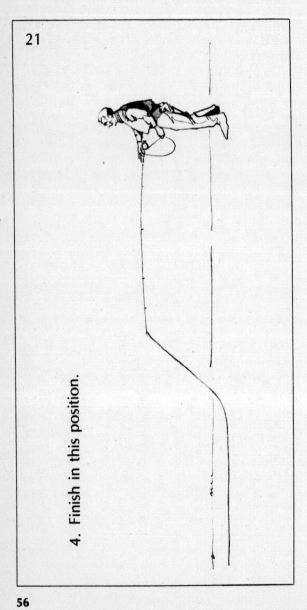

21

4. Finish in this position.

you, let the line go with your line hand. Practice will help you develop the timing to shoot the line—you must let go at a fairly precise moment with your line hand.

When you have practiced shooting line with a single backcast, you can practice lengthening your line while false-casting, letting out line on each forward cast. When false-casting and when shooting line, it is not necessary to keep the fly line held under the rod-hand forefinger, because you will be controlling it with your line hand. When fishing, however, it is helpful to put the line under your rod-hand forefinger at the completion of a cast. This finger will control the line by either holding it tight when fishing the full length of line or by letting line be pulled under it as you retrieve line with your line hand.

Roll Cast

To execute a roll cast, which is a valuable cast to know, you are casting without a full backcast. This comes in handy if you're on a stream where trees or bushes don't allow enough room for a full backcast. With thirty feet (nine meters) of line in front of you, raise the rod slowly from horizontal to the forty-five-degree angle behind you without picking up the line. Stop in this position. There should now be a semicircle of line behind the rod and slightly off to the outside. Then in a swift, smooth motion, return the rod to the horizontal position in front of you, stopping it abruptly. The line should have rolled in a big loop and landed once again straight out in front of you. Keep practicing this until it feels comfortable. Then practice it at different line lengths.

This is very basic casting instruction, designed to get you on the stream fishing. Whenever possible, seek personal instruction from a good caster. You will discover subtleties and refinements as you progress as a caster, and don't be afraid to break any "rules" of casting you've read

Casting

here or elsewhere if doing so increases your casting efficiency.

If you remember that it's a matter of timing, and that you have to adjust the timing and power to how much line you're casting, you'll be able to fly-cast efficiently. A half an hour of practice a couple of times a week will help tremendously while you're learning to fly-cast.

Line-Mending

Line-mending is the manipulation of your fly line on the water after you've made a cast. Basically, a line mend is a partial cast—instead of picking up and moving the entire line and fly, you are only moving a part of the line behind the fly.

The reason that you mend line is to speed up the float of the fly, to slow it down, or to keep the fly floating naturally at the speed of the current.

To mend to the left, hold the rod horizontal, and make a brisk circular motion to the left. To mend to the right, do the same thing in the other direction. In either case, the result should be a curving line from the rod tip to the end of the line.

When fishing, if you mend in an upstream direction, you slow the fly up. If you mend in a downstream direction, you speed up the drift of the fly. To best understand the dynamics of line-mending, try it on stream with a highly visible floating fly and observe the effect of your line-mending on the fly. How much and how often you mend line to keep your fly drifting properly depends so much on current speed and length of cast that on-stream practice is the best way to learn how to do it. You can't practice on a lawn or dry ground, because there is far less tension between the line and ground's surface than there is between the line and water's surface.

When you are on the stream, remember that at the completion of each cast you should place the line under your rod-hand forefinger. The line that you retrieve with your line hand while fishing may be allowed to trail in the current or it may be held in wide loops in your line hand. If held in the line hand, be sure to hold the loops loosely to avoid tangling them. When you want to reel in excess line, do so by holding the rod handle with the fly line that is going on the spool passing under one of your fingers. As you reel with the other hand, keep tension on the line as it goes onto the reel spool, spreading it evenly on the spool. If the line goes on loosely and unevenly, it will tangle on the spool.

4 Trout Streams

It may seem hard at first to look at a trout stream and figure out where the fish are in the stream. But once a little experience is gained, "reading water" begins to make sense and it can become fascinating. The ability to observe the physical features of a stream and then to judge how these features will affect trout is the basic task involved in reading water.

With some experience you'll be able to look at a stretch of stream and see a whole story unfolding before your eyes. You may see a little eddy of water behind a midstream rock and know that eddies like that often collect all manner of trout food and that usually there's a trout holding nearby, perhaps in the deeper water at the edge of the eddy. Some streams are more difficult to read than others, and some conditions (high water or low water, for example) can make reading a stream difficult. But a basic understanding of what a trout requires from a stream will provide you with an approach to reading water.

The primary requirements for survival of a trout are food, shelter, suitable water temperature, and suitable oxygen content in the water. Each of these requirements will affect the position a trout takes up in a stream.

Food. In a good trout stream, a trout doesn't have to travel far for nourishment. Some food forms occur in a stream in different places and at different times, and when they do, these foods may draw fish to them. For example, during a hatch of mayflies, immature flies (or nymphs) will normally be swimming from the stream bottom to the surface, where they will hatch into adult forms. Trout usually will be feeding both on the rising nymphs and on the winged adults on the surface. If the hatch is heavy enough, it will draw trout to it, and you will see the riseforms of the fish feeding on the mayflies. There is little problem here in deciding where to cast your fly.

When there is no hatch activity, trout will feed on the food that comes by their normal holding position. In most trout streams this means baitfish that swim too close to a trout or immature aquatic insects crawling about on the stream bottom or dislodged from their stream-bottom holds and floating helplessly by the trout in the current.

In times of low light—evening, night, and morning—trout will sometimes actively look for food, usually baitfish, in shallow-water areas. They will move out under the cover of darkness into riffles and the tails of pools in pursuit of food.

Shelter. A trout's shelter, or its holding lie, is normally located near some form of cover. This cover is the trout's protection from its predators. Some common forms of cover are undercut banks, trees or other objects that have fallen into the stream, in-stream rocks, and deep water. In any case the cover must protect the fish.

Shelter usually also includes a current slower than the main flow of the stream, because it requires less energy for the trout to hold in the slower current. But a holding lie is usually not far from the main current, because it must be nearby to a food supply. In a fast-flowing stream where there is little cover and few areas of slower current, trout are often found holding near the stream bottom, because in this way they can avoid the swifter currents above them. Depressions in the stream bottom, for example, often hold trout in such streams.

Water temperature. Water temperature affects where you'll find trout because trout are always seeking water temperatures that are most suitable for them. A stream thermometer is used to measure water temperature. On a warm day, when the water is low and the sun hot, the areas of a stream that are shaded will have cooler water. Incoming springs or spring-fed feeder streams will add cooler water in the hot months and warmer water in the cold months.

Trout are cold-blooded; their metabolism is affected by

TABLE TEN: **THE EFFECT OF WATER TEMPERATURE ON TROUT**

Water Temperature	Trout Activity	Fishing Tactics
33–45° Fahrenheit (.6–7.2° Celsius)	Body processes including digestion are slowed. Less energy is used to obtain food. Fish seem unwilling to pursue flies.	Important to place flies directly in front of fish. Fish will not move much to take a fly. Nymphs or drys best methods. Split-shot aids in slowing down nymphs.
46–65°F (7.8–18.2°C)	Body processes are accelerated. More energy is used. Digestive enzymes work more rapidly. Appetites are increased. Trout are quite active.	All methods—drys, wets, streamers, nymphs—work well, especially with a hatch. Trout will actively chase streamers or bucktails.
66–67°F (18.9–19.4°C)	Most active temperature. Digestion rapid. Appetites are large. Trout feed heavily.	All methods—drys, wets, streamers, nymphs—work well. With or without a hatch, trout will actively pursue moving flies.
68–69°F (20–20.5°C)	Trout are not quite as active as during temperature range directly above. Feeding activity is good, but usually some hatching activity is needed to move fish.	Drys or nymphs work best. Wets and streamers will still take fish, but not as well as at cooler temperatures.

70–72°F (21.1–22.2°C)	Trout activity is slowed. Temperatures nearing upper limit of good trout fishing. Fish unwilling to spend energy pursuing food.	Drys are best method. Trout unwilling to move very far to take a fly. As with cold temperatures above, flies must be put directly in front of fish.
72–74°F (22.2–23.3°C)	Feeding activity very reduced. Fish usually only willing to take food that is easy to obtain, which means surface feeding. 74°F (23.3°C) is upper limit of good trout fishing.	Drys only. Hatch or spinner fall practically a must.

the temperature of the water they are in. At ideal temperatures for fishing, the metabolism of a trout speeds up and the fish's requirement for food is greater than at other temperatures. While this doesn't mean that the trout go into a feeding spree when the ideal water temperature exists, it does mean that they are more inclined to feed actively and fairly unselectively.

Table Ten (pp. 62–63) shows the effect of water temperatures on trout and suggests fishing tactics for different temperatures. It was compiled for this book by Ed Van Put, a New York State fisheries technician and fly fisherman who has studied water temperatures and their effect on trout.

Oxygen content of the water. The oxygen content of the water will noticeably affect where you find trout in certain situations. Usually this becomes important in the summer months when the water is likely to be low, warm, and low in oxygen in some areas. At this time, fish may be drawn to areas below riffles or to areas of broken water because the fast churning of the water in such areas serves to oxygenate the water.

There are many other variables, of course, that will affect where you'll find trout in a given stretch of stream and how active they may be. For example, trout seem to avoid direct sunlight and to be most active during times of low light, which may include heavily overcast days. But the basic stream profile provided here, which considers the trout's needs and the physical characteristics of the stream, is a beginning toward effectively reading water. Once you've gained some experience astream, you'll be able to recognize the other variables and, with common sense, judge how they may affect trout.

5 Trout

THE FOUR MAJOR TYPES OF TROUT FOUND IN streams are the brook trout, the brown trout, the rainbow trout, and the cutthroat trout. While there are other trout species that inhabit streams, most trout-stream fishing is done for these four species. A fifth quarry sought with similar tactics as trout in some parts of the world is the grayling. This chapter gives brief information about each of these fish.

Brook trout (Salvelinus fontinalis). The native range of the brook trout is eastern North America from the state of Georgia to the Arctic Circle, and it has been introduced elsewhere in the United States, Canada, and South America. While technically not a member of the trout family (it is a member of the char family), this fish is commonly referred to as a trout. It has white-tipped fins, blue-and-red and sometimes yellow spots along its flanks, and the belly is often orange (see Color Plate One). The brook trout prefers colder water than the other trout species discussed here, and it is generally both shorter lived and smaller in size. Most anglers also consider the brookie easier to catch.

Brown trout (Salmo trutta). While the native range of the brown trout is Europe, it has been introduced throughout the world, being introduced to the United States in the 1880s. It has become a favorite quarry of the fly fisherman, and it is usually considered more difficult to catch than the other trout species. It is generally a golden brown with black spots along its flanks. Occasional bright-orange or red spots are sometimes present along the flanks of the brown trout (see Color Plate One).

Rainbow trout (Salmo gairdneri). The native range of the rainbow trout is western North America, and it has

Trout

been introduced elsewhere in the world where favorable conditions exist. The rainbow has black spots and a usually distinctive red band running laterally along its flanks (see Color Plate Two). It is popular among fly fishermen for its fighting qualities, being a long-running fish when hooked and also a frequent jumper.

Cutthroat trout (Salmo clarki). Like the rainbow trout, the cutthroat is a native of western North America. It has not been introduced to as many different areas as the rainbow. The cutthroat has black spots along its flanks and a distinctive red or bright-orange slash below each side of its jaw (see Color Plate Two). While the cutthroat is not as active a fighter as the rainbow, it is an excellent fly-rod quarry.

European grayling (Thymallus thymallus). The European grayling is found in many of the same waters inhabited by trout in Europe, where it is fished for with techniques similar to those used for trout. It is readily identified by its sail-like dorsal fin (see Color Plate Three), silver flanks, and gray-blue or gray-green back. In many places in Europe, anglers fish for grayling after the close of the trout season in the fall, thus extending their stream-fishing season.

6 Trout Food

IN MOST TROUT STREAMS, THE FOUR IMPORTANT kinds of trout food are aquatic insects, terrestrial insects, baitfish, and crustaceans. Their relative importance as food forms for trout varies from stream to stream and during the course of the season in a particular stream. Careful observation helps you to discover which form the trout may be feeding on at a particular time, and thus which form your fly should imitate.

Much has been written for anglers about these food forms, about imitating them, and about fishing their imitations effectively. Entire fishing books, for example, have been written solely on aquatic insects, and even on a single kind of aquatic insect. The information contained in this chapter is designed to give a very general overview of the behavior and characteristics of each of these four food forms. Wherever possible, I have avoided the use of scientific terminology in favor of the terms commonly used by anglers.

Aquatic Insects

There are four types of aquatic insects found in most trout streams that are important food sources for trout. These aquatic insects are mayflies, caddisflies (also called sedges), stoneflies, and midges. Each is classified as a separate taxonomic order by entomologists.

These aquatic insects occur in a variety of sizes and colors, and the following descriptions of these insects only covers the behavior and characteristics that each group of flies displays as a whole.

Mayflies (Ephemeroptera). In America the term mayfly

Trout Food

refers to any member of the Ephemeroptera order; in Europe the term mayfly refers to two species of Ephemeroptera that hatch in the spring: *Ephemerella danica* and *Ephemerella vulgata*. In this book I will use the term mayflies as it is commonly used in America: to refer to members of Ephemeroptera.

Mayflies are the best-known trout-stream insects to anglers, and there are many species present in streams. Each species becomes most important as trout food at a specific time of the year. The life cycle of the mayfly includes three basic forms: nymph, dun, and spinner. The nymph is the immature form that lives underwater. The dun and spinner are winged adult forms.

The mayfly nymph commonly lives on the stream bottom. Most mayfly nymphs have three tails; all have six legs, segmented abdomens, and thoraxes that are thicker than the abdomens. Some are rather squat and chunky,

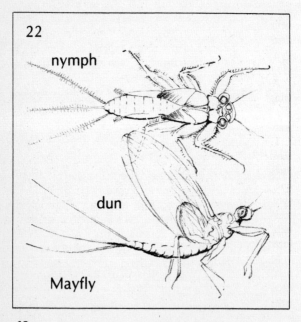

22

nymph

dun

Mayfly

while others are fairly long and slim. The mayfly normally lives as a nymph for a period of about one year.

Mayfly nymphs are available to trout when they are crawling around the stream bottom or when they become dislodged by the current from their hold on the bottom. They are most important as a food form, however, when they are swimming up to the surface to hatch into the dun form. Characteristically, an entire population of one species of mayfly in a stream hatches within a period of a few days or a few weeks, although some species hatch over a period of many weeks. This hatching period usually occurs daily and at the same time of day. The Hendrickson mayflies, for example, usually hatch every day between 1:30 P.M. and 4:00 P.M. for about two to three hours in April, May, or June.

During a hatch the nymph swims to the surface, breaks through the surface film, splits its nymphal exoskeleton, and emerges on the surface as a winged adult. The first winged adult form (or dun) usually rests on the surface, being carried along by the current, until its wings have dried and hardened and it is able to fly away. During the nymph-to-adult transition, the mayflies are quite vulnerable to trout.

Almost all mayfly adults have three tails, two large wings, and two small wings. All have six legs. Their bodies are usually long and slim, and when they rest on the water's surface the wings are held almost vertical.

The dun flies away to nearby trees and shrubs. Here most species stay for a period of about twenty-four or forty-eight hours. During this period the dun goes through one further metamorphosis, molting into a spinner. The spinner resembles the dun, except that it is normally slimmer in the body, the wings become translucent, and the tails become longer and more delicate. The spinner is the form of the mayfly that mates.

Mating may occur at any time of the day, but most mayfly species seem to mate in the late-afternoon or early-evening hours. The male and female spinners fly from the trees and congregate over the stream, usually over riffles,

Trout Food

and it may look like a cloud of flies, all bobbing and weaving in the air. Here the males fertilize the females. Sometimes you can see the conspicuous egg sac at the end of the female's abdomen. Normally they first congregate at treetop level, and then they slowly descend to within a few feet of the stream. Most females dip to the water's surface to oviposit. After mating, the flies often fall spent, usually with their wings in a spread-eagle position, to the water's surface, where they float along motionless—these flies are dead or dying. They float along freely, and trout usually rise to them leisurely. The fall of spent adults is called a spinner fall.

Caddisflies (Trichoptera). Caddisflies are the second type of aquatic insect that is important as food for trout. On many American streams they seem to be supplanting the mayflies as trout food, and perhaps this is because they appear to be hardier insects than the mayflies, more able to adapt to the modern ecological changes in many streams.

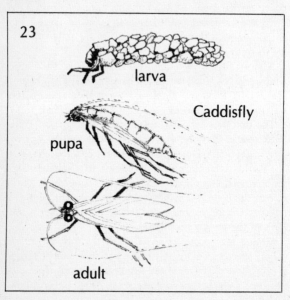

23

larva

Caddisfly

pupa

adult

Aquatic Insects

Unlike mayflies, caddisflies have no nymph form. Instead they have a larval and pupal form as immatures. While some caddisflies are free swimming in their larval stage, most of them build an encasement around themselves for protection. This case may be of tiny sticks or sand or other stream-bottom debris, and the larva stays inside, poking out to move around or to obtain food. Trout will sometimes consume the complete case for the nourishment of the larva inside.

After the larva pupates, the insect is ready to emerge. It leaves the case and rises to the surface. This form is called the pupa. The pupa, like the mayfly nymph, is often eaten by trout as it rises. Most caddisflies seem to rise by means of a gaseous "bubble" that helps float them as they swim to the surface. At the surface the pupa emerges as a winged adult (sometimes after drifting for a distance under the surface), which seems sometimes to pop out of the water quickly, bounce on the surface a few times, and then fly away. Many caddisfly-adult imitations are most effective when skittered or bounced across the surface to imitate this behavior.

The adult caddisfly has six legs, two long antennae, and four wings (two pairs). The wings lie over the back of the fly in a tentlike configuration when the insect is at rest.

The adult caddisflies mate over land, and like mayflies, they may fall spent to the stream's surface. The tentlike wings of the spent caddisfly usually project delta style, not quite spread-eagle like the mayfly.

While the egg-laying mayfly is not often available to trout in a stream, the egg-laying caddis often is. Some species, for example, will bounce on the surface, then free-drift, then bounce more to dislodge their eggs in the water, which excites trout into taking the fly. Other caddisfly species will land on the surface, swim to the bottom to oviposit, and then swim back to the surface. When they get back to the surface, they free-drift just under the surface film for a little ways, then pop out of the surface and fly away. Trout can feed fairly leisurely on these flies when they are free-drifting after laying their eggs.

Trout Food

Stoneflies (Plecoptera). Not long ago the general impression among anglers seemed to be that stoneflies were mainly important in the trout streams of the American West. While they are extremely important in those regions, especially the huge Western stonefly (sometimes called the salmon fly), stoneflies are present and important in many trout waters beyond those of the Rocky Mountains and American West Coast.

The life cycle of the stonefly resembles that of the mayfly: it has a nymph and adult form. The nymph has two tails, six legs, and it is generally quite flat. Like the mayfly nymph, it is available to the trout while it is crawling around the stream bottom or when it has become dislodged from its hold on the bottom and is carried along by the current. Unlike the mayfly, however, when most stoneflies are ready to hatch, they migrate to the shoreline and crawl up on streamside rocks or logs or onto the streambank and hatch while they are out of the water. The

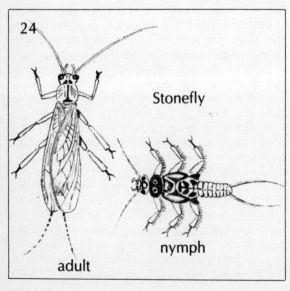

24

Stonefly

nymph

adult

shoreward migration of the stonefly nymph is a prime time for the trout to feed on it.

The adults of the stoneflies become important as trout food if they are blown onto the surface after hatching or if they somehow accidentally fall onto the water—stoneflies are clumsy fliers, and this happens often. They are most important in their adult form, however, during mating, after which they fall spent to the water. The females are also available during oviposition, when they may bounce violently on the stream surface, usually in riffles, to deposit their eggs in the water.

The stonefly adult has four wings that are held on top of each other, flat along the back, when the fly is at rest.

Midges (Diptera). Midges are perhaps more important as trout food than many anglers suspect. They may hatch year-round and may be a staple for trout in many streams. Perhaps it is their generally small size that makes anglers overlook them to a large degree.

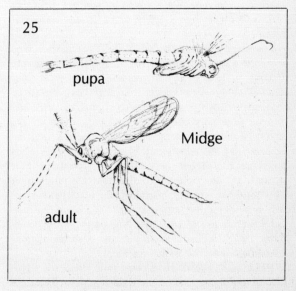

25

pupa

Midge

adult

Trout Food

Midge adults have six relatively long legs, no tails, and two wings that are set at an angle similar to those of a housefly (midges and houseflies belong to the same order of insects).

The life cycle of the midge resembles that of the caddisfly—it includes a larval, pupal, and adult stage. The larvae live in the stream bottom, and when they are ready to hatch they rise to the surface, where they hang suspended as they struggle to break through the surface film and emerge from their pupal skins as winged adults. Trout usually feed on midges during this emergence process, and midge imitations are often effective when fished in or just under the surface film.

Terrestrial Insects

In addition to the aquatic insects, trout will feed on landborn insects that happen to fall into the stream. These insect forms include ants, crickets, leafhoppers, grasshoppers, and other insects likely to be found near trout streams.

Terrestrial insects are generally high-floating when they are in the water, and most terrestrial-insect imitations are designed to float. Except on very windy days, most trout that feed on terrestrial insects do so near the streambanks, because that's where the insects most often occur. While summer is usually considered the time of year to fish terrestrial imitations, some terrestrials, such as ants, are available to trout year-round. However, summer is when there are the largest populations of terrestrials near streams, and the time of day that they are most active (thus most likely to end up accidentally in a trout stream) is from midmorning until evening.

Terrestrial insects, once they land on the water, sometimes struggle violently to get out, and in such situations you should fish your imitations accordingly.

A common occurrence on some trout streams is a proliferation of flying ants on the water's surface. These are

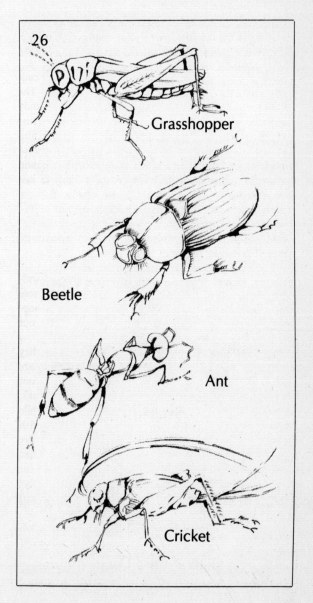

26

Grasshopper

Beetle

Ant

Cricket

Trout Food

the spent adults that have grown wings to mate and have happened to fall into the stream after mating. Trout may rise very selectively to these winged ants, and the trout's feeding behavior resembles their behavior when they are feeding on spent aquatic insects.

Baitfish

A portion of a trout's diet consists of the baitfish found in the stream. Although large trout are most likely to eat these small fish, I have caught many smaller fish on baitfish imitations. Imitations of baitfish are not exclusively "big-fish" flies.

Baitfish found in trout streams fall into two broad categories: free-swimming and bottom-dwelling baitfishes. The first kind, the free swimmers, are the small trout and minnows, such as dace, that swim at various depths in the

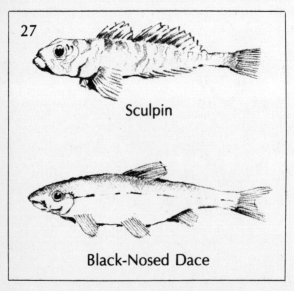

27

Sculpin

Black-Nosed Dace

stream. They are generally slim, and many of the free-swimming species have a dark lateral stripe on the flank. Bottom-dwelling baitfish, such as sculpin and darters, live among the rocks on the bottom of a stream, darting out to ambush their food. Bottom-dwelling baitfish normally have large heads and large pectoral fins designed for quick bursts of speed. They are usually squat, with mottled coloration for camouflage on the stream bottom.

Freshwater Crustaceans

This group of organisms can be a very important food for trout in some streams. Included here are crayfish, scuds, and cressbugs. Crayfish seem to occur in a variety of trout-stream types, and evidence of their presence is often given by a bleached claw along the stream. Crayfish look like little lobsters, and trout will pick them off the bottom and eat them, exoskeleton and all. An interesting characteris-

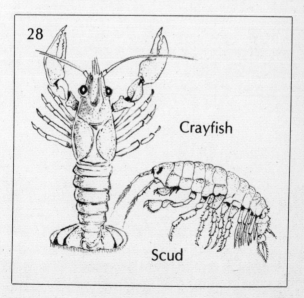

28

Crayfish

Scud

Trout Food

tic of the crayfish is that it propels itself along backward (tail first) when threatened.

Cressbugs and scuds seem to occur most often in weed-filled streams, where they live among the weed growth. In streams where trout are accustomed to eating these crustaceans, the fish will root around in the weeds to dislodge them and then eat them as the current takes them along.

While there are foods other than the aquatic and terrestrial insects, baitfish, and crustaceans that trout feed on, these groups represent the main sources of nourishment for trout in most streams. Trout may feed selectively on specific forms within these groups, and you must choose the appropriate size and color of fly to imitate these forms.

7 Trout Flies

IF YOU SPEND TIME WITH FLY FISHERMEN, sooner or later you're bound to hear someone refer to good old so-and-so who only fishes with one fly pattern in one size and catches more fish than anyone else. You'll probably also hear someone insist that a slight change in the body color of a certain fly pattern makes the difference between catching fish and not catching fish.

Generally speaking, a selection of trout flies such as the one presented in Table Eleven should outfit you for most trout-stream situations. None of these patterns are exact imitations; instead, they are impressionistic. They are suggestive of certain shapes and lifelike qualities of the food forms they imitate. These flies are shown in Color Plates Four, Five and Six, and all but one are standard fly patterns available at most fly shops or through mail-order tackle houses in the United States. The exception is the Wright's Royal, developed by Phil Wright of Wise River, Montana. I have included it here because I have found it to be an extremely versatile and effective pattern. A fly tier should be able to tie this (and the other patterns in the selection) from the information given in Table Eleven and the photographs in the color plates. This is a basic selection of versatile patterns, and certainly there will be other patterns you will need or want to try out. Your collection of flies may easily extend far beyond those listed here. Whenever fishing a new trout stream, or even when fishing your favorite stream, try not to miss an opportunity to ask other fishermen what patterns they find effective at certain times.

Trout flies are conventionally divided into the following categories: wet flies, dry flies, nymphs, streamers, and bucktails. Dry flies float; the other types sink. Wet flies are

TABLE ELEVEN: A SELECTION OF VERSATILE TROUT FLIES

Fly Pattern	Description	Recommended Sizes	What It Imitates
Adams	gray body, grizzly hackle-point wings, mixed dark-brown and grizzly hackle and tail	#10–#18	mayfly dun adult, caddisfly adult, some terrestrials
Black Ant	black body, black or dark blue-gray hackle (also effective in rust and cinnamon)	#10–#20	ant
Deerhair Beetle	dark-brown or black deerhair body	#14–#20	beetle
Tan Caddis	olive-green body, tan hackle-fiber wings, tan hackle (also effective in dark brown and gray)	#12–#20	caddisfly adult
Light Cahill	cream-tan body, lemon wood-duck flank-feather wings, light-tan hackle and tail	#12–#18	mayfly dun adult

Red Quill	brownish-red quill body, wood-duck flank-feather wings, dark blue-gray hackle and tail	#12–#18	mayfly dun adult
Gray Midge	gray body, blue-gray hackle	#16–#20	midge pupa and adult
Royal Wulff	peacock-herl and red silk body, dark-brown hackle, white calftail or bucktail wings, brown calftail or bucktail tail	#10–#18	some terrestrials, mainly an attractor pattern
Wright's Royal	peacock-herl and red silk body, brown elkhair wing, dark-brown hackle	#10–#18	some terrestrials, mainly an attractor pattern
Rusty Spinner	rusty body, dark blue-gray tail, polypropylene wings (also effective with dark blue-gray, olive, or sulphur body)	#12–#22	mayfly spinner adult
Leadwing Coachman	peacock-herl body, dark mallard-quill wing, dark-brown hackle and tail	#8–#14	some immature aquatic insects
Black Woolly Worm	black chenille body, red wool tail, grizzly hackle (also effective in assorted color combinations)	#4–#12	some immature aquatic insects

Table Eleven (cont.)

Fly Pattern	Description	Recommended Sizes	What it imitates
Tan Caddis Pupa	fuzzy tan body, some fibers left long for legs	#12–#16	caddis pupa, freshwater shrimp
Gold-Ribbed Hare's Ear Nymph	tan-gray body, gold ribbing, dark mallard-quill wing pads, dark-brown hackle and tail	#8–#16	mayfly nymph
Montana Nymph	black hackle-tip tails, black chenille abdomen and wing case, yellow chenille thorax, black hackle legs	#4–#12	stonefly nymph
Marabou Streamer	gold Mylar body, black marabou wing, grizzly hackle (also effective in assorted color combinations)	#2–#14	free-swimming baitfish, trout fry
Muddler Minnow	gold Mylar body, squirrel-tail underwing, turkey-quill overwing and tail, clipped-deerhair head with some fibers left long over back	#2–#14	bottom-dwelling baitfish, stonefly nymph, grasshopper when fished as a dry fly

Trout Flies

generally suggestive of subsurface insect forms. Dry flies imitate food forms that float. Nymphs imitate immature forms of aquatic insects. Streamers and bucktails imitate baitfish (streamers have feather wings; bucktails have hair wings). You will sometimes hear a fly referred to as an attractor pattern, which means that the fly doesn't imitate a specific food form but is designed instead to attract a trout's attention and stimulate the fish to strike.

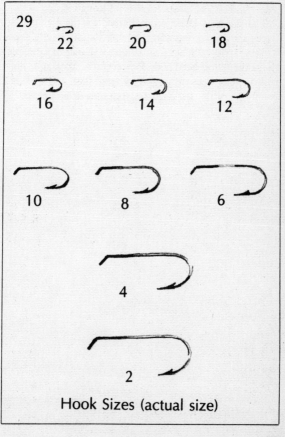

Hook Sizes (actual size)

Trout Flies

The size of trout flies is expressed by the size of the hooks they are tied on. Most hooks for trout flies today are designated in even sizes, with #2 (larger) through #22 (smaller) the sizes most commonly used. Hook sizes larger than #2 are 1/0, 2/0, 3/0, and so on, and they are generally used for salmon and saltwater fishing. Hooks as small as #24, #26, #28, #30, and #32 are available, but to my mind they are too small to be practical under most fishing conditions (I use #24 and #26 hooks in some special situations). Illustration Twenty-nine (p. 83) shows the actual size of hooks from #2 through #22.

The size of a hook is determined by the distance between the hook point and the hook shank directly above it. Some styles of hooks feature longer shanks or a different shape than illustrated here. However, the hook style illustrated is one frequently used for trout flies, and it gives a good idea of the standard size referred to by anglers.

8 Trout Stream Tactics

WHEN I FISH WITH MY BROTHER, I AM CON-
stantly reminded that you can never be too careful when
approaching a trout stream. Time and time again I have
kidded him about the way he'll frequently fall to the
ground and belly-crawl up to a favorite pool in order not
to scare the fish that are rising there, or the way he'll stalk
gingerly along a stream edge to get into position to make
the cast he figures will take a fish. God forbid that you
should get close to him while he's fishing to rising trout
if you're not prepared to fall to the ground, crawl up, and
whisper or use sign language. But he almost always
catches as many or more fish than anyone else, and often
the largest. He is not overly particular about the fly patterns he uses or about his leader taper. He is simply a
smart trout-stream tactician. He sees a rising trout or a
promising stretch of stream, lays a battle plan, and ap-
proaches the water always overestimating the trout's ability to detect his presence.

Fishing situations on a trout stream fall into two broad
categories: fishing for rising trout and fishing when no
trout are rising. This chapter gives some basic instruction
on how to fish under both of these circumstances. But, as
illustrated above, a deliberate and careful approach is es-
sential in either instance.

Fishing for Rising Trout

Fishing for rising trout is to my mind the most fun kind
of trout fishing. I'll often pass up trying many promising
pieces of water to find trout surface-feeding. Perhaps this
is because I love to see a fish rise to take a fly.

Tactics

When you locate a stretch of stream that has rising trout, the first thing you want to do is to try to figure out what the fish are rising to. Maybe you will have a good idea because someone has told you that the fish have been rising at that time of day to blue-winged olives or some other fly. But the best way to do this is to examine the stream surface to see if there are any flies on it that might be the ones triggering the feeding activity. Some of the flies may also be airborne, and if you can snare one out of the air for examination, this will help.

When you obtain a sample, you can quiz yourself. Is it a mayfly, a caddisfly, a stonefly? What color is it? What size? Then you simply choose the most appropriate pattern from your selection of flies. If you are stuck without the right fly, you may be able to trim a pattern with your clippers to an appropriate size and shape.

Along with this preliminary study you should also be watching the rising fish. Which ones are rising most frequently? Which ones will be easiest to cast to? Is it possible to fish for one of them that's a bit downstream from the others, which, if you hook it, can be played without scaring the others? Choose a specific fish to cast to.

Now that you've selected a fly pattern and a target, the next problem is to get into position to make a cast. You want to make a cast so that the fly lands at least twelve to eighteen inches (thirty to forty-five centimeters) upstream of the point where the fish is rising, and so that the fly will float without dragging (being pulled unnaturally against the current) over the fish. Is the sunlight throwing your shadow or the shadow of the line in front of you? Should you sneak up behind the fish and cast directly upstream? Should you circle around upstream and make a downstream presentation? Each trout stream is different, each fly fisherman has different casting abilities, and any given day astream presents numerous variables for you to contend with. You should try to avoid following any rigid set of rules about approaching fish, relying as much as possible on common sense.

If you cast over the fish and it doesn't take your fly and

it continues to rise, you may be using the wrong fly or the leader may be dragging the fly. Experiment with mending a loop of line in an upstream or downstream direction to avoid drag. Check your leader—are all its sections of the proper length? If not, take the time to rebuild it. If you feel sure that your fly is floating over the fish without any telltale drag, then try the same fly pattern in a smaller size. Then try a larger size. Then try a different pattern altogether. Try an ant. Try a caddisfly imitation and give it a little twitch—making it jump about its length—when it is about six inches (fifteen centimeters) upstream of the trout, then let it free-drift over the fish after the twitch. Try an attractor fly, such as a Royal Wulff. If these tactics don't work, try using a small nymph, letting it float over the fish an inch or two under the surface. You can do this simply by fishing it as though it were a dry fly; it will do the sinking on its own. Try the same thing with a caddis pupa.

If all of these things don't work, and the fish continues to rise, then you have found yourself an extremely finicky trout. Move on to another fish that might not be as selective. If the fish stopped rising, you may have scared it somehow, and you probably did if other fish nearby continue to rise.

If you are repeatedly unsuccessful, consult other anglers on the stream or in the area for advice on fly patterns and tactics. But chances are your failure is related to the very basic matters of approach, presentation, or fly selection. Try always to be thinking about these basics. The most successful anglers that I know seem to possess the ability to cut through all the intricacies of the sport to solve streamside problems with surprisingly simple solutions.

When a trout rises to your dry fly, you should strike to set the hook. Don't overreact. Merely raise the rod tip quickly, extending your rod arm up, and tighten the line by pulling down with your line hand. It doesn't require force to set the hook in a trout's jaw; usually all you need to do is to pick up the slack line quickly and establish tension on the line and leader.

Tactics

Fishing When No Trout Are Rising

If you arrive at the stream and don't see any fish rising, it doesn't mean that the trout aren't feeding. They could be and probably are feeding quite actively under the surface. Most trout feed most of the time under the surface on immature forms of aquatic insects. But, of course, a trout feeding on nymphs would probably not pass up a minnow that carelessly swam too close to the trout, and it might even rise to a floating insect on the surface. If you take the water temperature of the stream before you start fishing, you'll get an idea of how actively the fish may be feeding below the surface.

There are two kinds of subsurface fishing: nymph fishing and streamer fishing. In either kind of fishing, you must put the fly you're using in those areas of the stream that you have recognized as holding lies. The fly should travel through the holding lie and along that edge of the holding lie that is adjacent to the main current, which is the area that the trout probably turns its attention to when it's hungry. Most of the time this means putting your fly right next to the streambank. If you need to use a sinking-tip line or to attach one or two split-shot or other kind of weight to the leader, go ahead. The casting may be awkward with weight, but the important thing is to get your fly to the fish because, unlike a rising trout, these fish are not being drawn from their holding lies to a source of food.

When you're fishing nymphs you are trying to do just what you did with dry flies, only under the surface. That is, you're trying to get a drag-free float close to a trout. A fly can drag unnaturally under the water as well as on the surface. You don't have the advantage of knowing exactly where the trout is—this you'll have to judge by reading the water. You also don't know what the fish may want to eat —but it is probably not as selective as it would be when rising to dry flies. Try each of the basic nymph types in your fly box: mayfly nymph, stonefly nymph, and caddisfly pupa. Nymph fishing is often a trial-and-error method.

Fishing When No Trout Are Rising

Probably the most effective way to fish nymphs is with an across-and-down approach. Beginning at the head of the stretch of stream you plan to fish, cast across stream into a holding lie and drift the fly through the holding lie and along the edge of the holding lie, letting the line swing around and downstream until it is straightened out below you. Let it hang for a moment, then cast again. Before each new cast, take a step or two downstream. You should try not to miss putting your nymph in any area that might hold a trout.

As in dry-fly fishing, when your nymph is in the water you may have to execute a series of line mends. This mending process is designed to keep the fly in a free-floating drift. If you mend a loop of line upstream, it'll give slack to keep the fly from being dragged unnaturally through the water. If you mend a loop of line downstream, it'll allow you to pull in unnecessary slack, keeping a relatively straight line between you and the nymph.

When a trout takes a nymph, it usually does so casually. You should watch the point where the line or leader enters the water, and if it jumps or hesitates slightly, lift the rod tip sharply to set the hook. It might be a fish or it might be a stream-bottom snag, but you have to strike to find out. Some strikes by trout are very subtle on nymphs, and there probably will be plenty that you'll miss noticing altogether.

Sometimes, just before a hatch occurs, nymphs will be actively swimming toward the surface. If you know from experience or from sound advice that a certain hatch is about to occur, try fishing the appropriate nymph imitation at middle depth, giving it an occasional upward dart by manipulating it with the rod. When the hatch is in progress to the point that the nymphs are emerging as winged adults, these same trout will probably start feeding on the surface as well as on the nymphs that are still ascending to hatch.

If you have no idea what nymph pattern to choose, one way to find a suitable choice is to turn over stream-bottom rocks to see if there are any nymphs or larvae clinging to

Tactics

them. If they have some nymphs or larvae on them, simply choose a suitable imitation—a mayfly, caddisfly, or stonefly in the appropriate size and color.

A streamer or bucktail that imitates a free-swimming baitfish is almost always fished with a retrieve motion to make it look like a swimming or injured baitfish. You should fish this type of subsurface fly in the same areas that you fish the nymph, but instead of free-drifting it, give it an occasional dart or jump. Try to visualize what a wounded baitfish might look like and try to simulate it. A wounded baitfish is often an easily obtained meal for a trout. The same across-and-down approach that is used with nymphs may be used with these flies. It is often effective to make an occasional free-drifting presentation.

The imitations of bottom-dwelling baitfish may be fished near the stream bottom. It is most effective to let these flies free-drift along the bottom, as with nymphs, but giving the fly an occasional darting motion. These imitations may also be fished with a wounded-baitfish retrieve.

With both the free-swimming and bottom-dwelling baitfish imitations, after you have let the line straighten out downstream of you, retrieve the imitations in to you. Also, when fishing either type of baitfish imitation, experiment with various retrieves. Try fast retrieves, slow retrieves, stop-and-start retrieves, and a free drift once in a while.

The streamer represents a food form that the trout must attack quickly because it might get away, and strikes on streamers are often hard. Usually the trout will hook itself —it'll be on the line almost before you know you've had a strike. When the fish is on, raise the rod and tighten the line; there's no need to strike back.

When there are no rising fish, you can at times fish effectively with dry flies. An attractor pattern, such as a Royal Wulff or a Wright's Royal, cast into holding areas along the banks or behind midstream rocks or even into riffles, may produce exciting fishing. Many smaller streams that don't have large populations of aquatic in-

Fishing When No Trout Are Rising

sects to produce rises of trout are best fished with dry flies. And on most streams in late summer, fish are quite often willing to rise to grasshopper imitations cast near the streambanks.

9 Playing and Releasing Trout

WHEN PLAYING A TROUT, YOU SHOULD LET THE fish work against the fly rod. After striking and hooking up, raise the rod tip so that the rod is at an approximately sixty-degree-angle to the water's surface. Retrieve excess line onto the reel. You should maintain a gentle arc in the rod, and when a fish runs or pulls against it, the rod will bend and recover.

If a fish runs strongly enough it will take line off the reel, so you must have the reel drag adjusted so that pressure is put on a fish pulling against it. The drag should be tight enough to keep the spool from overrunning when it gives line, and loose enough to let the reel give line instead of breaking the leader tippet or pulling the hook out of the fish's mouth.

Playing a trout is a give-and-take affair, but you should bring the fish in as quickly as the size of the fish and the strength of the tackle allow. This is especially important if you plan to release the fish, because an overtired fish has a small chance for survival when returned to the water.

You should have little difficulty in bringing in a fish under ten inches (twenty-five centimeters) quickly, pressuring it away from weeds, deadfalls, and other snags that might break the tippet. Larger fish, however, demand a little more care. The best way to bring in a large fish quickly is to exert pressure from side to side—that is, to either side of the fish's head. The fish has less strength to fight back in this plane, and you can put pressure on it in this plane by changing the direction of the rod.

Finding out when a fish is ready to be netted is a trial-and-error thing. When the fish appears to be ready, try to net it. If it swims insistently away, wait and try again. A trout will usually make a strong run when it first sees the

Playing and Releasing

net and you close up, and you should be ready to net it after this spurt.

The basic technique for netting a trout while you're wading in a stream is to hold the rod in one hand and the net in the other. Try to position yourself so that the trout can be slid downstream into the net by extending your rod over your head and behind you. Before the fish is to be netted, place the net underwater, letting the current unfold the net bag. Keep the mouth of the net underwater, and when the fish can be slid over the mouth of the net, raise the net smoothly. Lead the trout head first into the net. Avoid any quick jerking or stabbing motions with the net.

If you haven't got a net, you may want to wade ashore while playing a large fish, and when the trout is spent, ease it up onto the beach. Fish under ten inches (twenty-five centimeters) may not require a net, because they can be handled quite easily in the stream, if you either want to release them or keep them.

If you plan to release a large trout, it's a good idea to use a net. You can bring the fish in quicker, thus avoiding overtiring the fish. Holding the fish gently in the meshes of the net, twist the hook out with your fingers or, better still, with a pair of forceps. You can tuck your rod under your arm to keep it out of the way and free both hands.

It is extremely important that you avoid touching as much as possible any trout to be released. What may seem to be a relatively gentle hold to you may result in internal damage to the trout. If you have in some way damaged the trout's gills, or if there is bleeding in the gill area, the fish will probably die if released—if regulations allow, keep the fish if you decide you've damaged its gills. If a trout is hooked deeply in the throat with the fly, sometimes it's best to cut the tippet and sacrifice the fly to save the fish —the hook will eventually rust away or be dissolved by stomach acids.

If you plan to release a fish and you haven't got a net, bring the fish in close and take the leader tippet in your hand. Follow the tippet down with your hand until you

Playing and Releasing

can grasp the eye and shank of the hook firmly. Then twist or shake the hook free. If the hook won't come free, tuck the rod under one arm, and using two hands, hold the fish firmly by placing your thumb inside its lower jaw and your forefinger underneath it—a small trout's teeth usually allow a firm hold without cutting deeply. If you have a bandana or handkerchief with you, you can wrap it around your thumb to protect against being cut when using this technique with larger fish. You can then work the hook free with the other hand or with your forceps.

Most trout under ten inches (twenty-five centimeters) that are brought in quickly will dart off almost as though nothing has happened once they're released. Larger trout, however, often need time to recover after a fight. You can help a trout do this by gently holding the fish steady, upright in the water, facing upstream. When the fish is able to move off under its own power, let it go. While holding the fish, make sure that the gills are working—if they aren't you can aid this action by gently moving the fish back and forth into the current. All of this has to be done gently. If the fish doesn't require aid in working its gills, you need only to help it remain upright. Try not to hold it at all unless it needs help in staying upright.

Some trout will sink to the stream bottom after being released and hold there, resting. As long as the fish is remaining upright, this is okay. Keep an eye on it, though, to make sure it doesn't start to turn on its side. Usually it will soon scoot off.

10 A Trip Astream

IN THIS CHAPTER LET'S SPEND SOME TIME ASTREAM. Let's look at several fishing situations and see how the application of some of the techniques covered in this book help you catch trout.

You are fishing a small stream in the Blue Ridge Mountains of Virginia. It is May, so the water level is healthy, the stream runs cool, and the dogwood and rhododendron are in bloom. The stream, narrow enough to jump across in places, tumbles staircase fashion through a series of tiny waterfalls.

It's not hard to tell where to cast your fly. The fast water spills into little pools deep enough to provide shelter for the trout from osprey, raccoons, and mink. The fast water that pours into the pools carries food: immature forms of aquatic insects that have become dislodged as they crawl about on the stream bottom or as they cling to underwater rocks, terrestrial insects that have fallen from a streamside bush or tree onto the water, even small baitfish that have somehow gotten caught in current too swift for them. This is where the trout will hold and feed. Shelter and food are the important requirements that the little pools offer.

You cast your fly, a nondescript nymph imitation—a size 12 Gold-Ribbed Hare's Ear—into the fast water and let it be carried over the waterfall into a small pool, where the slowly churning current carries it about. You use a roll cast because the trees and shrubs are close to the stream bank and you need only cover about twenty feet with the cast. Suddenly your line jumps slightly and you raise your rod tip to set the hook on a plump, brightly colored native brook trout. You work your way up the splashing staircase repeating this simple tactic and you meet with repeated success.

Small-stream fishing rewards the angler who keeps a low profile and makes a good presentation to the holding water. In this instance, knowing where to cast and how to do it discreetly is more important than matching the hatch or using ultrafine tippets.

Later in the season you find yourself fishing the Battenkill in Vermont, a larger stream characterized by long, slick pools followed by shallow riffles. As it winds its way through a gentle New England valley, the Battenkill flows gracefully under red covered bridges and past staid white-clapboard farmhouses toward its junction with the Hudson River in New York State.

It's June and you arrive at the stream in the warm early evening, hoping to find trout rising to a hatch of mayflies in the long pools. But there are no rises, so you fish with nymphs and streamers in the pools and riffles. An hour passes with no success, not even a little strike or a snag on the bottom of the stream.

Where are the trout? you ask yourself. *Are there any trout in this river or is the "good fishing" here merely a hoax cooked up by the local chamber of commerce?*

You have worked downstream to the tail of a riffle—the spot where the current slows to form a pool—and there's a sudden, solid pull on your line. You're punished for your musing about local civic officials: Attention diverted, you miss the chance to strike back to set the hook. But now you're in business.

You cast upstream, still using the Montana Nymph that brought you the first strike, letting the fly and line sink and swing around to the spot where the riffle tail becomes the pool head. In the same spot as the first strike there's another pull. This time you tighten the line and raise the rod quickly: A proud fourteen-inch brown trout comes shortly to net. You take a second smaller fish from the same spot using the same technique before moving downstream to another riffle where more trout await. You've found the trout in the safety and comfort of the deeper water feeding on food washed downstream to them by the riffles, just the same kind of spot as on the Blue Ridge Mountain stream, only on a larger scale.

Here, even though it was a little bit by accident, you discovered where the fish were feeding and concentrated your fishing at those spots. The upstream cast gave the line and leader enough time to sink to the right depth, and when the line began to swing out below you the nymph was lifted upward and across the current a bit, and it was probably taken for a stonefly nymph attempting to crawl to shore to hatch.

Now it is August and you are on the Henrys Fork of the Snake River in Idaho. You have made the drive down to Island Park from your headquarters in West Yellowstone to try this legendary stream.

You had called ahead to see what was hatching and were told that the *Tricorythodes*—tiny, white-winged, black-bodied flies—were hatching and that the best fishing was to the spinner fall, beginning at eleven in the morning. Use size 22 to 24 imitations, you had been told, and 7X tippets.

As you wade out into the even flow of this remarkable spring creek, there are rainbow trout rising everywhere. The river is so large and relatively easy to wade that each one of many anglers has his pod of rising fish to cast to.

For years you had heard that the Henrys Fork was a very difficult stream. Finding a suitable spot you discipline yourself to watch the trout rise, to choose a target, and to look for a rhythm in your target's feeding pattern so you can place your fly on the water at exactly the right time.

Well, here goes! you think, and false cast out enough line to place the fly several feet above your target, directly upstream. The fly lands and floats without drag over your fish. Nothing happens. The trout keep rising, keep sticking their snouts leisurely out of the water to feed, and you begin to worry.

Right fly? you ask yourself. *Yep, a* Tricorythodes *spin-*

97

A Trip Astream

ner, just what the fly shop recommended. Tippet and leader?
It's seven X and the fly is riding without drag.

You redouble your efforts, trying several different targets, but after an hour you have had only one false rise.

Discouraged, you reel in and start asking the questions again. Suddenly, you remember the trout stream back home, 2,000 miles away, and that when this happens on your stream, it is sometimes a masking hatch. That means, even though the *Tricorythodes* spinner seems the perfect choice, the trout may be taking a less abundant but more appealing fly.

You look down to the water's surface and see the profusion of *Tricorythodes* spinners. But, *there!* A larger spinner . . . *yes!* It's a rusty-bodied spinner just like the ones that mix with the *Tricorythodes* back home. You scoop it from the water's surface and examine it closely. Choosing a match from your fly box, you replace the 7X tippet with 5X (the new fly is a size 18) and look up for a target.

The same trout are still rising. Again you cast just upstream, and *bingo!* The rainbow takes and is off and running. The strong sixteen-incher takes line off your reel again and again before you bring it in and carefully release it.

For the next hour you are a happy angler, catching and releasing your share of the rainbows until the feeding activity tapers off.

On the Henrys Fork you learned that trout and insects behave similarly everywhere and the skills and knowledge acquired on one river can be applied to another river anywhere in the world. Everyday astream is part of your education as an angler. On the Henrys Fork, if you had been fifty yards upstream, perhaps all the fish would have been taking *Tricorythodes* as predicted and not the rusty-bodied spinner; that's one of the variables that makes some rivers so challenging. But you also learned that a healthy dose of common sense and independent thinking brings rewards in a sport with as many variables as fly-fishing for trout.

11 Trout Stream Etiquette

DUE TO THE GROWING POPULARITY OF TROUT fishing, the quality of the angling experience depends on people and their behavior more today than it probably ever has in the past. In spite of the quality of a stream, its environs, and the fishing itself, a day fishing can be unpleasant because of discourteous anglers you may encounter. Generally speaking, the fishermen (fly fishermen and otherwise) that you see on the stream are friendly and courteous, but it only takes a minority to create unpleasant fishing conditions.

There is a traditional etiquette to observe while you're fishing a trout stream, and following it will help insure that you won't ruin another's fishing. The basic rule of trout-stream behavior is not to spoil the water that another angler is fishing or plans to fish. For example, don't wade through a pool that another angler is fishing. If you want to fish downstream from him, determine if he's fishing in an upstream direction or not. If you can't tell, ask. If you are fishing and moving quickly and you come upon another angler in the stream, circle around him in such a way that you don't disturb the area he is fishing. But first ask if he's moving upstream or downstream and if it's okay for you to circle around and continue in the direction you are fishing.

When fishing in an area where there are other people fishing with methods other than fly-fishing or where there are nonfishermen using the stream or its banks, watch your backcast. People who are not familiar with fly-casting may not know that your backcast will loop out behind you and they may walk into it.

Etiquette not only applies to other anglers and people near the stream, but to nearby landowners as well. If you

99

Etiquette

are unsure of the rules of access to a particular stream or stretch of stream, inquire with local authorities or a nearby landowner. You will need to know if you are allowed to fish there, where you can park your car if you're driving, and whether you can cross private property to reach the stream. In some cases, such inquiries result both in permission to fish and valuable local advice on fly patterns, tactics, and best spots to try your luck.

You should also familiarize yourself with any special rules or regulations regarding a specific water you plan to fish as well as general angling laws that apply. Such rules normally appear in literature that is supplied with the purchase of a fishing license. It is your responsibility to know the laws governing the waters you fish.

Index

Boldface numbers indicate material in tables or illustrations.

AFTMA. *See* American Fishing Tackle Manufacturers Association

Accessories, 31–35

American Fishing Tackle Manufacturers Association (AFTMA), 8

Aquatic insects, 67–74
  Caddisflies, 70–71, **70**
  Mayflies, 67–70, **68**
  Midges, 73–74, **73**
  Stoneflies, 72–73, **72**

Backing to reel knot, 36, **37**, 38

Baitfish, 74–77, **76**

Basic cast, 48–57

Blood knot, 18, 39, **40**

Brook trout, 65, Color Plate section

Brown trout, 65, Color Plate section

Casting, 47–59. *See also* Basic cast, False-casting, Line mending, Roll cast, Shooting line
  holding rod for, 47, **47**
  line hand in, 47
  rod hand in, 47

Clippers, 32

Cutthroat trout, 66, Color Plate section

Double surgeon's loop, 18, 39, **41**

Etiquette, 99–100

European grayling. *See* Grayling

Index

False-casting, 48–52
Flashlight, 34, 35
Floatant, 33, 34
Fly box, 31–32, 34
Forceps, 32–33, 34
Freshwater crustaceans,
    77–78, **77**

Grayling, 66, Color Plate
    section

Harvey, George, 18, 22
Hat, 34, 35
Hooks, 83–84, **83**
Hook sharpener, 34

Improved clinch knot,
    44, 46
Interlocking loops, 18,
    39, **43,** 46
    making loops for, 39,
    42, 46

Knife, 33, 34
Knots. *See* Backing to
    Reel, Blood knot,
    Double surgeon's
    loop, Interlocking
    loops, Nail knot,
    Turle knot
Kreh, Lefty, 35

Leaders, 17–27, 33
    braided-butt, 23, 26
    color of, 27
    "hard nylon," 18
    length and size of,
        17–18, **19**
    on sinking-tip line, **20,**
        23
    removing coils in, 27
    size and strength of,
        23, **26**
    "soft nylon," 18
    straightener for, 23,
        33, 34
    tapers, 18, **21, 22,**
        24–25
    tying, 18
Lines, 8–14
    abbreviations for, 9,
        11, 12
    backing, 10, 14
    color of, 12
    density of, 11–14, **11**
    fly, 8
    labeling of, 14, **14**
    maintenance of, 12–13
    shooting-taper, 12

Index

storage of, 13
tapers of, 8–10, **10**
weights of, 8, 9
Line mending, 58–59

Nets, 34, 35
Netting trout, 92–93,
     Color Plate section
Nail knot, 38, **38**

Orvis Company, The, 23,
     31

Playing trout, 92–94

Rainbow trout, 65–66,
     Color Plate section
Reeling in line, 59
Reels, 14–17
   automatic, 15
   capacity of, 16–17
   drag systems of, 15
   maintenance of, 16
   mounting on rod of,
     16, 17
   multiple action, 15
   putting line and back-
     ing on, 17

reversibility of, 15–16
single action, 15
spare spools for, 16,
     34
Rods, 2–8
   action of, 5–6
   bamboo, 2, 6–7
   boron, 3
   boron/graphite, 3
   carbon-fibre, 2
   carbon-graphite, 2
   fiberglass, 2–3
   graphite, 3
   kits for building, 6
   length of, 3–4, **5**
   line weights for, 4–5, **5**
   maintenance of, 6–7
   storage of, 7–8
Roll cast, 57

Shooting line, 52–57,
     53–56
Split-shot, 33
Sunglasses, 34, 35

Tactics, 85–91
   approaching trout, 85
   avoiding drag, 86–87
   choosing flies, 86,
     89–90

Index

fishing for rising trout,
85–87

fishing when no trout
are rising, 88–91

nymph fishing, 88–90

positioning for dry-fly
fishing, 86

streamer fishing, 88,
90–91

striking fish, 87–90

Terrestrial insects, 74–76,
75

Thermometer, 34

Trout, 65–66. *See also*
Brook trout, Brown
trout, Cutthroat
trout, Rainbow
trout

Trout flies, 79–84, 80–82,
Color Plate section

Trout food, 67–78. *See
also* Aquatic insects,
Baitfish, Freshwater
crustaceans, Terres-
trial insects

Trout streams, 60–64
food in, 60–61

oxygen content of, 64

reading water of,
60–64

as trout habitat, 60–64

shelter in, 61

temperature of, 61–64,
62–63

Turle knot, **45**, 46

Twistons, 33, 34

Vest, 35

Waders, 27–31
bootfoot, 27–28

drying, 30

fit of, 28

hip boot, 27

repairing, 31

soles of, 28–29

storage of, 30

stockingfoot, 28, 29

Wading, 29

Wading staff, 29, 34

Wright, Phil, 79